Freddy M

Fall from
Grace

Photograph opposite.
A young Freddy Maertens with his mother who, sadly, has passed away since this book was originally published in Belgium.

Maertens, Freddy
Adriaens, Manu
Freddy Maertens. Fall from Grace/Freddy Maertens, Manu
Adriaens, translated by Steve Hawkins – Hull:
Ronde Publications, 1993 – 236p.; 20cm
ISBN 1 898111 00 6

Title of original Dutch language publication:
Freddy Maertens: 'Niet van horen zeggen' as told to Manu
Adriaens.
© 1988 Standaard Uitgeverij, Belgiëlei 147a, Antwerpen,
Belgium.

Front cover photo: Photosport International
Back cover photo: Maurice Terryn
Photographs reproduced with kind permission of: Photosport
International, John Coulson, The Press Association,
Associated Press, Hulton-Deutsch Collection, Freddy
Maertens family collection. Particular thanks to John Pierce,
Photosport International.

Printed and bound by:
Clifford Ward & Co. Ltd.,
55 West Street, Bridlington, East Yorkshire YO15 3DZ

Typesetting by:
ABM Typographics Ltd.,
Unit D, Gothenburg Way, Sutton Fields, Hull HU7 0YG

ISBN 1 898111 00 6

Contents

Foreword

In the world of cycling, when a rider becomes a champion his decline, when it inevitably begins. is often a gradual and graceful process. For double world champion Freddy Maertens this was not the case.

In 1976 Freddy achieved a record-breaking 55 victories including 8 stages of that year's Tour de France and the World Championship at Ostuni in Italy. Three years later he won only two races. Yet in 1981 Maertens returned to the heights to gain 5 stage wins in the Tour that year and once again he became World Champion, this time in Prague. That was the last race of any consequence he ever won. He continued to ride until 1987 but his form was never the same.

Throughout Freddy's career he was dogged by rumour and speculation regarding the unpredictability of his performances. This mystery will unfold as you read on and I will not spoil the ending for you.

As an Englishman, looking on at the then closed world of professional cycling, I was intrigued to discover the true story behind his fall from grace. More especially since, for me, Maertens inspired my own humble cycling career. I was a fan. In a sport dominated by the brilliant Eddy Merckx, Freddy never ducked the challenge that faced him. This tenacity was to serve him well in future years as you will later learn.

I only saw Maertens race once. That was the Kellogg's City Centre Criterium in Manchester. I travelled the 100 miles or so that night to see Freddy in the flesh. He raced poorly that evening: finishing well down the field. It was a sad sight.

In the spring of 1990, on a business trip to Paris, I stopped off in the West Flemish city of Bruges where I obtained a copy of Maertens' autobiography 'Niet van horen zeggen.' The only problem was that it was written in Dutch, a language of which I had little or no knowledge. At this point I enlisted the help of translator Steve Hawkins, whose painstaking and meticulous work on this version has meant that Freddy's autobiography can now be appreciated by English language readers. Steve like myself is a mad keen cycling fan. This publication has been a labour of love for us both.

John Hunter, Ronde Publications

We made a start on it together on the first Monday of January 1988. 'It's time it happened,' said Freddy on the telephone on the Sunday evening when I rang him up to fix the exact time for our appointment the following day. By 'it,' he meant writing the book, the idea for which had been running through his head over the past couple of years. The first stone of our working relationship had been laid one Tuesday afternoon in October 1986. A few weeks before then, I had written a report for the newspaper I was working for at the time about his parents-in-law. The basis for the article was that two world champions had married into their family; Maertens and Jean-Pierre Monseré. I had promised to return the photograph that appeared with the article to them and I delivered it to Freddy at his house in Rumbeke that Tuesday. We talked for a while and as someone else was visiting at the same time, he started telling a few strong stories about the notorious 'end-of-season race' at Putte-Kapellen (notorious for the way the riders let go of themselves afterwards) which was being held that day. He had consciously refused to ever take part in it and as he talked about it I listened on, both interested and amused.

'You ought to put your recollections down on paper,' I suggested.

'Just say the word,' Freddy replied straightaway. 'We'll do it together.'

I thought he was joking. I know I'd interviewed him a couple of times before, but it never went any further than that.

'Do you mean that?' I asked.

'Of course I mean it,' he answered. 'But first I want to use the 1987 season to free-wheel my way out of the sport.'

And so we started out on it together on that first Monday of January 1988. During the hours-long conversations we had at his house, he would tell me everything he had to say and the tape recorder between us would record it. I was allowed to ask him any question I liked, he had assured me, he would answer everything. He kept his word and gave honest answers, banging his chest whenever he dug up incidents in which he had been at fault. Throughout the chronological recall of his cycling career, we would regularly go more deeply into sensitive areas (result-fixing, doping etc.) that others prefer to keep cloaked in secrecy.

'For whom will I be telling all of this?' Freddy asked me before we had begun the book. 'Did they ever spare me?' That may sound like revenge, but it isn't the case. That's not the way Maertens is. As he says in the last chapter: 'I'm not someone who would dirty my own nest. I don't want to give a kick in the teeth to the sport for which I have much to thank. It's just that after all the things that have been said about me in the past, it is finally time for 'my' truth to be heard.

After consultation between us, it was decided to leave one or two fragments which had been recorded out of the book, just so as the privacy of a number of people would not be threatened. It was certainly never the intention, then, to turn this book into a sort of score-settling exercise. What finally went into it was given much consideration, even though it will still be hard to take for a few people. However, if life isn't that wonderful, you don't go around saying how fantastic it is. Why must silence always be golden?

During our hours-long conversations, I came to respect Freddy Maertens as a person much more than I did before. The same goes for his wife Carine, who stayed in the background throughout his career and even now prefers shuffling quietly into the lounge keeping us topped up with coffee and following our conversation at a distance. Sometimes she would go along with my express request to add things during the sittings and would have her say.

One day, on arriving at the Maertens household for the umpteenth time, I said, 'I feel just like Lomme Driessens coming to your house every day.' To which Carine said, 'Yes, but at least you don't tell me how I should make minestrone soup.' All three of us had to laugh at that. Then there was the nine-year-old Romy, sitting in the corner of the room stroking her black cat.

You know, I reckon I'm going to miss it a bit.

Manu Adriaens

1 As long as the nest is warm

It has been said that an artist must have had an unhappy childhood to be able to have got as far as he has. This isn't really necessary to become the world champion cyclist – I'm the living proof of that. I didn't grow up in a poor family, but we weren't well off. This meant that I had to start work at a young age. At home we made a living in two ways; my father ran a laundry and my mother worked in her grocer's shop every day. In the evenings when I got back from school I had chores to do in both places. In the laundry I did what my dad told me to and in the shop it was my job to bring empty bottles into the store, fill the shelves with new stock and help with the maintenance. I saw how busy my parents always were and didn't find it at all strange to have to give them a hand. Beside that though, I had enough spare time to enjoy my teenage years in a carefree way and to do what I wanted most; to go cycling. My parents never for one moment stood in the way of my becoming a cyclist, so I've got no right at all to say I had an unhappy childhood.

I was born on February 13th 1952. Michel Pollentier, whose name you'll find many times in this book since much of our careers have run parallel to each other, was born only a few kilometres away in Keiem, exactly one year to the day before me. That may be purely coincidence. Beside the fact that we both became cyclists there is no magical link behind it. I don't believe in astrology. My star sign is Aquarius and I sometimes have a look at my horoscope in the paper for a laugh, but I've never let it influence my life. Anyway, the only thing that Michel Pollentier and I have in common is that we both have self-employed parents (his father owned a garage). Apart from that we have completely different characters. When it comes down to it Michel can be more headstrong, while I tend to let things blow over more quickly. For instance, when we rode together at Flandria and played practical jokes on each other I could cope with it better than he could. In spite of that, though, we've always got on well with each other, even during the period when our cycling careers took their own separate directions. We still keep in touch regularly. I ring him up and say *'Tjelle'* and I immediately hear the reply *'Mette'* from the other end of the line.

My birth was a difficult one. My mother worked in her shop until almost the last day, and the long pains of childbirth wore her out. When I eventually appeared I immediately contracted bronchopneumonia, a serious lung infection. After ten days my mother was allowed to take me home, but when my condition failed to improve there was no alternative but for me to be taken back into hospital. I had to stay there for about six months. Not only did I end up in an incubator with breathing apparatus, but every day, Sister Angelique or one of the others would give me six injections in my little bottom. I suppose you could say that that was my first experience of doping.

During that period in the clinic my father was allowed to come and visit me at night via a special entrance. On one occasion it was just as well, since the oxygen infusion I was receiving needed to be replaced. However the clamp was twisted and the night nurse couldn't undo it. In a state of panic she phoned my father. Although it was absolutely freezing outside, he didn't waste time putting on a shirt or jumper and leaped immediately into his car and rushed to the hospital, which was only a stone's throw from our house. When he couldn't undo the clamp either, he drove at full speed to the owner of the garage he used in Nieuwpoort, knocked him up out of bed and asked him for a monkey wrench and finally managed to get the thing disconnected. He arrived just in time as I'd started to turn blue through lack of oxygen. I've never been closer to death than I was then.

Because I continued to suffer from the lung infection after I was taken home, one day my father decided to take me to a little chapel in Wulpen. Just next to it there was a water well in the middle of the fields. To anyone who just happened to be passing, the water would look really dirty, but once you had removed the frogspawn that was floating on top, it was the clearest water you could ever imagine. Some of it was sprinkled on me while I was there and my father took some home with him to boil my baby-food in. It certainly seems to have helped, since just as everyone was thinking that I'd never be rid of the condition and would always be a sickly child, I recovered.

Although I don't believe in astrology I really do believe this story about the spring water which my parents were to tell me later. Of course, the sceptic may question where the boundary between belief and superstition lies, but the facts speak for themselves. They had tried everything to cure my fever in the hospital without success, yet what medical science couldn't cure, the pond in that field was able to. A customer in our laundry just happened to give the tip to my parents, and they took this advice, probably thinking if it didn't work no harm had been done. My parents have always been religious and so have I. Like my three brothers I received a Catholic education and I am not in the least embarrassed about that. Cyclists very rarely talk about religion or anything connected with it. Although there is a Sporta-pilgrimage organised in various provinces before the start of each season, it may be that it is just down to folklore and simply a chance for everyone to have a bit of a get together. If I had the chance I would always attend mass on the Sunday during a stage race. When Pollentier and I won the Baracchi Trophy together, the most famous two-up time trial, in 1976, we had attended mass that morning. Only a few in the peloton ever did that. If some riders wanted to poke fun at me for that, well let them – each to his own beliefs.

My father's father was a plasterer. Dad himself started a laundry on the Albertlaan in Nieuwpoort-Bad. The washing was collected from those people who wanted it doing. The busiest time of year was, of course, the tourist season in the summer when the hotels and guest houses were taking in holiday-makers. We would often have problems with the neighbours. Because my father sometimes worked right through until after midnight and the machines made a bit of a racket, they threatened to take him to court for causing a noise nuisance. It would have been difficult, however, for my father to have finished all his work by ten o'clock at night. To avoid any further trouble he moved the family home to Lombardsijde, to his father's house, where he had a completely new set of machines installed. At the front of the building my mother opened a grocer's shop. She did this with an eye to later life, as with four children my parents wanted to provide a secure future. Later on, in 1966, the business was expanded to become a newsagency as well. This part of the business was to become my responsibility when I ended my studies at Ostend College.

As far as character is concerned I am more like my father, taking my fighting qualities, forcefulness and my ability to push myself to my limits from him. It was he who moulded me. From the moment I took up cycling he kept a close watch on me. He wanted to make a decent rider out of me whatever it took and I am still grateful to him for the way he tackled it. I was allowed to train as often as I liked and the same went for my work, but going out in the evening was something that I could only dream about. While the other lads of my age went off eyeing up the local beauties at Westende-Bad, I was tidying up the shop or working the ironing machine in the laundry. On one occasion I trapped one of my fingers in the roller of a machine and it didn't seem to concern my dad too much that I might have to have it amputated. His steely temperament was later to stand him in good stead in local politics. As a public spirited man, he was asked to stand for the local interests party which had a tendency towards liberalism, and because he was self-employed he felt at home with them. He was the sort of character who really needed his own business and I could never imagine him working in a factory.

My mother has always worked just as hard as my father. Very rarely did I see my parents have their evening meal before ten o'clock in the evening. After she had closed the shop, my mother had several tasks to undertake for the next day such as cleaning the meat slicer, scrubbing the floors, displaying new stock, marking the prices and so on. Then there were always things to do in the laundry. On more than one occasion my parents didn't even get to bed because they had so many things to get ready. The whole work process in the laundry was very labour-intensive. After the sheets had been taken out of the enormous washing machines they needed to be rinsed, wrung out, put into the driers, hung outside and finally folded. When I was little I once crawled into one of the driers and switched it on. Luckily my father realised what had happened in time.

I was certainly no classic example of obedience. When I was four I jumped onto my tricycle, still wearing my pyjamas, and set off in the direction of the football pitch about 400 metres from our house, where a match was being played. After an intensive search they found me with my pyjama trousers caught up in the chain, black all over and it meant I had to get straight back in the bath out of which I had just emerged. Later on I would put other things into the bath tub, such as my father's rabbits. I also went round from door to door with a birdcage, trying to sell our canary. It was a success, but that was probably more to do with the ten franc spot

4

prize I was also offering. Afterwards, the people who had bought him from me brought him back, to the great relief of my parents. Once, with the lads who lived in the neighbourhood, I scooped up horse muck from the street, wrapped it in paper and put it through the letterbox of someone who wasn't exactly one of my favourite people. I'd also play at ringing people's doorbells and running away. In reality, none of this was anything more than mischief in the traditional sense.

Sometimes, I would ride the much bigger bike – which I had received in exchange for my three-wheeler – to the local football pitch and ride onto the pitch itself while a game was going on.

"I bet you daren't get the goalkeeper's shorts off him," some of the older lads once challenged me.

"I bet I dare," I boasted, then I sneaked behind a goalpost without being noticed, quietly stole up until I was right behind the goalkeeper and suddenly yanked his shorts down. The other lads were howling with laughter at my nerve.

Sometimes I had to face the consequences of my own pranks. That is how I came to be badly burned on one of the irons in the laundry. I was playing with a screwdriver and put it into an electric socket. The force of the electric shock I received sent me flying off the table onto which I had clambered and that was what actually saved me. On another occasion I sat behind the steering wheel of our car and turned the ignition key. As it was in first gear, the car went jerking down the hill. Fortunately for me, my father once again spotted what had happened, came running after it, jumped into the car next to me and managed to bring it to a halt in time.

I inherited the other side of my character from my mother: not seeing the bad side of things straightaway, placing too much trust in people and being gullible. Anyone who knows me well knows how concerned I have been about my mother's health. She now has to undergo dialysis treatment twice a week. That doesn't mean, however, that I could be called a mother's boy when I was a youngster. I wasn't spoiled and all four children were equal before the law. It would have been impossible to have been spoiled by her anyway, as because she was so busy, we were mainly looked after by my grandmother.

Mario is two years younger than me, Luc three years and Marc, the *baby* of the family, seven years younger. As the oldest I have always felt responsible for them to a certain extent; for the first three years of Marc's professional cycling career, for example, I was able to give him lots of help since we rode for the same team.

I got my first real bike through my cousin, the cyclist René Maertens. My parents paid for it in part but René certainly had a large share in it as well. Before that, though, I did have a bike with balloon tyres. My grandfather taught me how to ride time trials on it. I always had to ride over the same course and he would let me know whether I had beaten my previous best by checking on the second hand of his wrist watch. He would push me to my absolute limit and actually drove me a little mad. If anyone fanned the competitive flames in me in my early years it was him. He drove into my head continuously that I must try to do my best in all circumstances. He knew what he was talking about as he had once raced himself. His son Maurice, my father's brother, had also been a rider. It is not surprising that you often hear that mothers are against their sons taking up cycle racing. However, my mother didn't seem to object. My grandfather, with his fervent encouragement, sowed the seeds of competitiveness in me. She was only too happy that he was able to spend so much time with me, as she was up to her neck in work.

From the age of six I would go and watch the races that my cousin René from Koksijde was riding in. I was even allowed into the changing rooms if I wasn't thrown out by one of the other riders, as I was once by Tuur De Cabooter. René was already a professional rider by then and whenever I could, I went to races with him. I carried his bag and polished his bike. He had a good sprint but didn't train very hard. His training runs usually involved riding to a given destination and leaving it at that. If he had applied himself a bit more he would have definitely gone on to achieve more in his career. In those days there was a rider called Bernard Maertens from Nieuwpoort and although he was no relation, I often went along with Eric Van Roey, who was one of his most fervent supporters, to see him ride.

Although we lived in Lombardsijde, I went to the infant school in Westende. I did this because one of my mother's relatives was a teacher there, and since there was a shortage of local school-children, his job was under threat. When the weather was nice he would come and collect me and we would go to school together on our bikes. If the weather was bad, he would take me in his car. I was an above average pupil and was given a mark of around eighty percent each year. In the first and second years our teacher was a certain Mr Ingelbrecht who had a reputation for being very strict, and as I was a distant relative of his, he would sometimes pay extra attention to me. Two brothers called Bloese took the remaining years, one taking the third and fourth, the other the fifth and sixth years.

My lower secondary education was at the Sint-Bernardus College in Nieuwpoort. I always liked going to school but from my first year at Nieuwpoort I had to work very hard at my studies. Often I would get up very early on the day of an exam so that I could revise in peace and quiet. In particular I had trouble with maths, I just couldn't get the hang of it, and this was to become more significant in my later life when numbers and figures began to play an important part in my business affairs. When I was at Sint-Bernardus College I liked to play football and my favourite position was goalkeeper. You are on your own in goal, and in this respect it is similar to riding a bike. Later on, when as cyclists we would play football matches during the winter period, I would usually keep goal. I was even signed to SC Lombardsijde, the local club in which my father was involved in a management role for a short while. My brother Luc made it to the first team and Marc was a star performer in the junior teams.

I never became a footballer though. During 1966 I began to ride in the Criterium of the Westhoek, a series of criteriums held in West Flanders for boys who hadn't yet ridden in BWB (the Belgian Cycling Federation) races. Before that, when I was twelve, I once took part in a time trial over one and a half kilometres in the village of Ramskapelle and I won against boys who were much older than myself. I had been told that the race was open to all-comers but once I had crossed the line the organisers informed me that it was only for boys who lived in Ramskapelle and I therefore had to relinquish my trophy. It was the first victory I had taken away from me and unfortunately it was not to be the last.

When I decided to enter for the Criterium of the Westhoek at the age of fourteen, my father backed my decision. He merely said, "Once you've started you are going to have to go through

7

with it." In actual fact he was delighted to have a son who wanted to be a cyclist. He kept a very close eye on me, and other people have often said to me, "You always seem to have needed someone who kept you on a tight rein: first your father, then Lomme Driessens."

I wouldn't like to say that I agree with that, but what is true is that my father has always given me a great deal of support. However, from the earliest days I realised only too well just what I had to do. When I went training I didn't need my father with me: I went out on my own, the way it should be. Sometimes on an evening I would go for a ride on my own as a form of relaxation but on one occasion I had good reason to regret it. In 1969, when I was already a junior, I had got to know a girl called Marcelle who came from Nieuwpoort. She worked as a waitress in a snackbar at one of the campsites in Lombardsijde. Somebody must have informed on us since on one evening, when we were cycling along hand in hand, we were confronted by my father.

"Go straight home!" he yelled, whilst throwing in a few choicer expletives.

On arriving home, I discovered that he had literally sawn my bike frame in half. He was absolutely beside himself with anger to the extent that he had a bit of a heart flutter and we had to send for the doctor. A week later, he bought me a new bike.

I went to Onze-Lieve-Vrouw College in Ostend for my higher secondary education. Peter Caron, the director of the institute, was never much in favour of my cycling activities. When during 1969 at school I lost my wallet containing my identity card, my tram season ticket and my BWB licence, he decided not to return it to me until the cycling season had finished. His deceitful action didn't achieve very much though, as I applied for and received a new licence well before the end of the season.

I never finished my final year at secondary school. When I decided I'd had enough at Ostend my father said to me, "If you want to quit school to concentrate completely on cycling, I respect your decision. But you'll have to help us in the running of the business."

In practice, what this meant was that the paper round which until then I had only done during the school holidays, became my responsibility entirely. It was hard work but I enjoyed it. I would get up at half past five in the morning and most months of the year the job was finished by ten o'clock, although in the tourist season it would be nearer noon. The two jobs actually complemented each other very well since I had every afternoon free and could go training or compete in races. Even getting up early didn't worry me as if I went to bed early enough it was no problem and sometimes I was in bed by nine o'clock at night.

One of the reasons for the complete lack of top riders in Belgium nowadays is that young riders are too mollycoddled. They don't get up until nine o'clock to go training, completely missing the early morning when the quality of the air is at its best. It's no coincidence that the best riders of all time have, to a man, come from less well-off families. A background like something from 'Dallas' is no breeding ground for hard working *Flandrians*.

I used to struggle through the loose dune sand to the campsite, pulling a trailer behind my bike. I received plenty of pocket money for my job. Once, when a woman whose husband had been away all week, opened the door half dressed, I certainly had something to look at. I'm not making it up, it actually happened.

I've always liked the coast, but I realise that one of the main characteristics of people living along it is their jealous nature. If two restaurants are next to each other, each owner will count how many people are going into the other one. I now live near Roeselare but I only feel homesick for the sea in the winter; certainly not for the part of the year when people are fighting each other for a square metre of beach. It is particularly beautiful in winter, calm, and with a special charm if there has been a slight frost. Golden Boot award winner, the late Wilfried Puis who came from De Haan, still regarded himself as *a son of the coast* whilst playing football for Anderlecht. I also found that there seemed to be opposition to me because I came from the coast, while Eddy Merckx was from Brussels. I was not received by the King after either of my World Championship victories and to this day I do not know why. Perhaps it has something to do with my face. Yet no matter how far away from Brussels I live, in my heart I'm still a Belgian! At a later date, when I was a guest on Ro Burms' radio programme *'Kwistig met muziek,'* in the regular feature *De Hartewens* (The Heart's Desire), I was given a chance to apply for a reception by the King. I was assured in advance it was going to be arranged for me but I decided not to ask. If that was the only way it was going to happen I wasn't interested.

2   The Burgomaster's Prophecy

I made my debut in the Criterium of the Westhoek in July 1966, straight after the end of the school year. In the first race at Wulveringem I only managed to finish one of the eight circuits. It was the first time that I had ridden in the 'peloton' and I was scared stiff. Until then I had always trained on my own and riding in a group took a lot of getting used to. After the race, I wept with fear. I was only fourteen and at that time the upper age limit for riders in the Criterium was still eighteen – it was reduced later to sixteen – so many of the other competitors were much bigger than me.

One week later I took part in the race at Wulpen, the place where I had been miraculously cured when I was a baby. There was to be no second miracle that day, though, since I didn't win. However I did manage seven of the ten laps and in my third race in Alveringem I finished 7th of the 32 starters. From then on things went well: if nothing untoward happened I would easily be able to reach the finish, and challenge in the sprint for one of the top places. All of this was achieved on a bike my cousin René had got for me.

"If you can do well on a bike like that, you shouldn't have any trouble on a better one," was my father's opinion.

The bike was reasonable but it was a cheap one. When I go to youth-category races nowadays I'm amazed at the gleaming machines I see, some of which must have cost tens of thousands of francs. Sometimes I think they're convinced that the prize is going to go to the one with the most impressive cycle. They seem to have forgotten that a race is not a sort of *Miss Bike* competition, but a matter of pedalling as fast as you can. On that score my dad's way of thinking was right.

That first bike served me for the whole of the 1966 season and for the following winter as well. I experienced the thrill of winning during that first season, and what made it even better is that when it came, on September 26th 1966, it was in my own Lombardsijde – where my dad was one of the organisers. I knew the course like the back of my hand, which was a real advantage. In the pouring rain we had to cross some tramlines twice on each circuit, which increased greatly the danger of a crash. You had to show a bit of acrobatic skill at those points and I made the most of it.

In a way my friendship with Michel Pollentier dates from that day. We rode together at the front over the last few circuits until his back wheel suddenly slipped on one of the tramlines. I waited for him because I felt that the two of us together had a better chance of staying at the front. When it came to the sprint I wasn't afraid of him though, and at the finishing line I beat him easily.

Although we knew each other and sometimes went on training rides together, we didn't do each other any favours during a race. Michel's last race in the Criterium of the Westhoek in 1967, before he moved on to th juniors, was proof of that. In Veurne he rode virtually the whole race at the front. I was with a group of chasers who gradually got nearer to him and on the last straight cobbled section he came into sight. After a desperate effort I managed to get up to him and a few metres before the line I got past him. Afterwards his supporters whistled their disgust at me.

Wasn't it a bit soon, though, to be making deals about who would win? I knew only too well that even among the newcomers that sort of thing goes on all the time, but personally I find it terrible. In the youth-category you ride like mad for all you're worth! Whenever Michel was riding at the front with me he was certain of second place, whereas if it ended up as a mass sprint he'd finish nowhere. He knew then, that it was to his own benefit to work at making an escape. During the course of a race we would share all the sprint bonuses as that was only fair. In fact, if it had been up to me I would have probably let him win sometimes, but my dad would never allow it.

There was never any question of race-fixing between Pollentier, Norbert Lesage from Hooglede and me. They wanted to win just as much as I did, so there was always fierce competition; not least because Lesage would always ride on my wheel without ever doing his share of the work. That was the big difference between him and Pollentier and it really used to annoy me.

In 1967 my 12 victories made me the overall winner of the Criterium of the Westhoek, ahead of Hugo Vermeersch from Ostend, Robert Vanhercke from Adinkerke, Michel Pollentier and Norbert Lesage. The Dutchman Antoon Van Den Bunder, who later on as an amateur often used to be impressive during the important Belgian semi-classics, finished 15th that year. Looking back on it, I regard the Criterium of the Westhoek as a good training-school, especially since in those days boys could still race up to the age of eighteen. They had four years more experience than you did, but you could still beat them. As well as this, at that time there was no restriction on gear sizes, so gear ratios were a matter of personal choice. People have pointed out that apart from Pollentier and me, no other top riders have emerged from the Criterium of the Westhoek, and they're quite right. I can't really give a good reason why, except to say it's probably due in part to a lack of ambition. The only rider I know of who went on to do anything is Noël Vantyghem who won in 1964 and as a professional went on to win Paris–Tours.

In the nineteen seventies an even younger version of the Criterium, for the youth cycling circuit, was established. It was later banned by the Flemish Community Council and I can understand why. In my opinion, children of eight racing against each other is just a little too much, too soon. On the other hand, I find the BWB's decision to allow riders from its own 'boys' category to only race once a week more puzzling. The decision as to how often to race should come from the doctor whose supervision of all riders is compulsory.

I am of course no great fan of the BWB, for reasons which will become apparent during the following chapters.

As winner of the Criterium of the Westhoek, I was required to attend a reception at Lombardsijde on Sunday 17th December 1967. In the scrapbook I have from those days, the text of what Burgomaster Coulier said in his speech that day is typed out. The last paragraph reads:

"Freddy, never take winning for granted, but always remember that no matter how successful one may be, a sudden setback is sometimes unavoidable. When that happens it is difficult to climb back up the ladder. If, however, you show courage and sports-manship, then succeeding in doing that will have been the greatest achievement of your cycling career".

Neither Burgomaster Coulier, nor I as a fifteen year old, could have guessed at that moment how close to the truth those prophetic words would turn out to be.

3 The Work of a Maniac

When I switched from the Criterium of the Westhoek to the 'newcomers' category of the BWB in 1968, in reality it didn't signify a huge step up – just the opposite, in fact. Sometimes races were 70 kilometres long in the Criterium – in those days the distance raced wasn't limited either – while races in the newcomers category were always shorter. That was to turn out to give me a considerable advantage. Michel Pollentier didn't even bother with the newcomers, but went straight on to the juniors category.

That year I won 21 races and came second 18 times. When I was second it was usually Rino Vandromme from Kachtem who won the laurels. If I attacked and he got up to me, he very rarely took over any of the leading work. That's the reason he generally had the most strength left at the finishing line. Unlike his brother, Ludo, Rino never turned professional, he carried on as an amateur. That illustates the fact that he always took it too easy in the youth categories, where he never needed to demonstrate a will to win. I gained my revenge for all my second places by beating him in the West Flemish Championship at Sint-Denijs on June 16th. On the gently sloping road on the way to the finish I started the sprint from a long way out and he couldn't get past me. He was really annoyed with himself on that occasion. His reaction was understandable as in many other similar situations that's how he'd beaten me, but this time he was obviously over-confident. The great rivalry between us was also reflected by our clans of supporters. One of his brothers and one of mine once actually came to blows at Zwevezele, and when Vandromme and I crossed the line we got involved in the fracas as well. The outcome was that we both had to appear before the green disciplinary table of the BWB.

On July 7th I came 15th out of the 103 riders in the Belgian Championship at Tertre, Rino Vandromme finished the season top of the winnings table with 29, ahead of Noel Bosman from Chaumont-Gistoux with 25 and me with 21. On December 8th, back home in Lombardsijde, I was once again triumphant; this time when I became West Flemish champion. The celebrations were led by the *De Zeekust* cycling club, of which my father was the chairman, and by the *De Lombardenspurters* supporters club under the chairmanship of Suzanne Huwe. "Jack-of-all-Trades" Emile Broucke spoke these words:

"On the occasion of this reception, we would all like to say to you: stay modest, train hard, live soberly, follow your father's advice and always be grateful to your parents. You're standing on the first rung of the ladder which will lead you to glory: make sure you don't fall off it . . ."

It would seem that, just like Burgomaster Coulier one year before, he possessed paranormal vision that day.

My debut season with the juniors in 1969 went better for me than my debut with the newcomers: I won 22 times. Ludo Van Der Linden was a real glutton that season with no less than 67 victories. I also took more second places than the season before with 28. At this point I would like to add that from the youth categories onwards I went to ride in all the Belgian provinces, even in Wallonia. This fitted perfectly into my father's strategy, who had made an extra financial effort to pay for all the long distance trips. I didn't meet many other riders from our area because it seemed that they preferred riding between the church towers near where they lived. What they didn't have that I certainly did was a clear idea of the quality of riders from other provinces. It was hardly a fluke, then, when I came in 4th in the Belgian title race on 13th July at Nandrin. Only Luc Pels, Ghislain Debuysschere and Johnny Soenens finished ahead of me. Afterwards however, all the journalists who were there described me as the most deserving man of the race. My father didn't make a fuss about the fact that maybe I'd been a bit impetuous. He would rather have seen a rider working hard but failing to win the championship than someone winning it on the sweat of others.

During that period Dr Jolie from Kortrijk took over my medical supervision. I'd heard that he was a specialist sports doctor and I wanted to meet him. His watchword was simple: train hard. Indeed alongside a necessary part inspiration, cycling remains above all *transpiration*. I almost said *trainspiration*. Because of this I always made sure my training distances were greater than race distances. At regular intervals Dr Jolie would also check my blood pressure and make sure that all the essential constituents were present in my blood. If there was a shortage of anything it would be replenished by vitamins or other supplements. As far as food was concerned I didn't have to pay particular attention to what I ate.

"There's plenty of time for that sort of thing when you become an amateur."

His viewpoint was that I had to get to know myself more. "As far as I'm concerned you can eat chips just before a race if you want to, Freddy," he said. "Just as long as you let me know afterwards how you felt during the race."

Roger De Vlaeminck claimed in his top years, *"I give my body what it wants."* I doubt that, though, and during the week leading up to Paris-Roubaix, he'd be best advised to avoid chips. There's also the story surrounding Michel Pollentier, who during the course of his career is said to have consumed kilos of chocolate. While that may be true, we should not forget that chocolate can have something of a stimulating effect. Just try drinking a cup of coffee and eating a piece of chocolate when you're really exhausted and you'll feel fitter straightaway. That's something you can't put down to coffee on its own.

I sometimes hear the physios of young riders claim; "Potatoes aren't good for a racer, it's best to give him spaghetti." You do need to eat potatoes sometimes to help make your bowels function properly. However the golden rule here is; as long as you don't overdo it, it's alright. Anything with *too* at the front (too much, too fat, etc.) is bad. Even *'tevreden'* – Dutch for content. If you become too content too soon you'll find it difficult to get really motivated.

When I say that a rider must get to know himself, it is particularly true during the time when he steps up from amateur to professional status. If you think you can make it as a team leader, try it for one year. If it doesn't work out during that year you need to have an attitude healthy enough to decide that you're better riding in the service of someone else. Much of the blame for the pretensions some first-year professionals have can be put down to their environment. Parents and supporters say things that put their heads in the clouds; "You can do it," they say to them, even though it's obvious they can't. Team leadership carries more with it than is obvious at first sight. The pressure is great, very great.

15

Beside training and a healthy diet there is a third important factor and yet it is the one which is often forgotten; rest. Young riders go on a training ride, come home and then go out somewhere else straightaway. I never did that. After training I used to laze on the settee for a while. I realise of course that I had to get up very early for my paper round, but to make up for it I used to have a nap in the afternoon.

Others who helped me in a different way at the start of my career, i.e. with my equipment, were cycle maker Johny Mahieu and his wife Jeanne from Oostduinkerke. They always made me very welcome. My brother Marc trained at Johny's as a cycle mechanic until we started our own Flandria shop in Lombardsijde in 1976. Unfortunately Johny took that very badly, and though I have been in contact with him since, he and my parents have never had anything more to do with each other.

A trusting relationship with your mechanic is absolutely essential. That was true in my case for Freddy Heydens in particular during my time with Flandria. Although Eddy Merckx had the reputation of being a stickler for equipment I was just the same; it's just that I didn't make such a show of it as Merckx who would sometimes sit fixing his bike in front of the T.V. cameras. One day, after I was married, I had been training in my new racing shoes. In the middle of the night I got up without being noticed to try them out again. I couldn't sleep because I wanted to be sure whether the shoe plates were mounted in the right place. My wife suddenly noticed that I wasn't in bed next to her and she came outside looking terrified. When she saw me sitting on my bike she quietly asked me if I'd gone mad.

I feel that if you don't get obsessed with the smallest details of your chosen profession, you're better off giving it up. Even when my saddle wasn't clean enough *underneath* for my liking, I would give it a wipe myself. Polishing my shoes during a stage race was also a job that I wanted to do myself in my room. It's the equipment that helps you win, so you have to treasure it. That's why the role of the mechanics, who often work until deep into the night, is so important. They have a great deal of responsibility during a long stage race, especially when the team-leader is near the top of the general classification. Among other things they have to examine is whether there are any tiny cuts in the tyres. In a time trial, it is the little things like that which can make all the difference between victory and defeat.

I was very particular about my handlebar tape. I wanted it renewed every day, just as I wanted new toe straps regularly and checks to make sure the spare wheels were in perfect condition. It was very rare that I had to get angry about things not being prepared the way I wanted them to be. A factor in that is that the personnel always had every incentive to do their work perfectly, since everybody got 10% of our earnings on top of their monthly wage. On occasions when they had put in some extra work I would give them a bit of pocket money. They knew that what was worth doing was worth doing well.

4 Carine

I was a second year junior in 1970. It was also the first season that I didn't have to worry about school work, and once I had done my daily paper round I could devote all my attention to cycling. It clearly had an effect on my results and I won 43 times that season, though I failed once again to land the national title. On Sunday August 2nd in Meulebeke, Karel Sels was able to capitalise on the personal battle Rino Vandromme and I were fighting out. Vandromme's race that day was entirely geared to what I did. Every time I attacked he would close down the gap without ever going to the front himself fearing that he would come off worse in the sprint. I was boiling over with anger and when I made my displeasure public after the end of the race, the neutrals in the crowd could see my point of view. It had been so obvious what had happened that I couldn't miss the chance of pointing it out to anyone who wanted to hear. I have often been accused of being too indiscreet and I have been told that I should think about things a bit longer before shooting my mouth off, but I think there are times when the truth needs to be told. That is simply the way I am: spontaneous. I would rather be open than a hypocrite; I would stand by all the things that I have said in the past and not take back a word.

It was at the end of 1970 that I got to know my future wife, Carine Brouckaert. It was Jean-Pierre Monseré, who became world professional champion at Mallory Park in Leicestershire, England that year, who introduced us. I had known Jean-Pierre for a little while and he was somebody for whom I had a great deal of respect, indeed I really looked up to him. Gradually we became firm friends, we would often go on training runs together and I would stay at his house. In November of that year it was Jean-Pierre who arranged for me to do my military service close to my home, since he knew Commandant Lierman. Thanks to this man I was posted to the barracks in Lombardsijde and after a short time I was transferred to the officer's mess in Middelkerke where I was provided with more facilities than I had had previously.

Although Jean-Pierre had a reputation of having a taste for the good life I know one thing; when you went on a training ride with him, it was flat out all the way. He was one of those people who took a devilish delight in forcing people on to the wrong foot by giving the impression that he didn't take his profession particularly seriously. In the summer he would set off to go training at six o'clock in the morning and would be back at home by nine. It was then that the riders he had arranged to go training with would turn up.

"I don't feel like going training today," he would then say, and in so doing, he was helping to continue the myth about him.

Just after the others had gone, however, he would change into his racing gear again and go out riding behind a motorbike for a couple more hours.

Had it not been for his fatal accident during the Annual Fair Grand Prix at Retie on 15th March 1971, we would have probably made a good pairing in the professional ranks. Although he was four years older than I was we got on very well together. Jean-Pierre was always pleased to see me, and his widow is still a close friend today. I can ring her up at any time of the day and if she can help me she will.

Annie Monseré and my wife Carine are cousins and were brought up together in Rumbeke, which is close to the town of Roeselare. When Annie's mother died at a young age Annie and her sister Christiane, together with their father, went to live with Carine's parents who also had two other children: Rik and Christine. Just for good measure, her grandmother lived with the family as well. All of this meant that my mother-in-law had a great deal of washing and cleaning to do, but she never complained and just got on with it. As they say in West Flanders: *'You don't die of work'*. My parents-in-law have had a unique reward for their hard work; they are the only couple in the world with two sons-in-law who both became world champion cyclists.

Carine was sixteen when Jean-Pierre, who was already married to Annie, asked her if she would like to go with them to the ball organised by WSC Torhout the following night. He had never actually been a member of my cycling club but had been invited along as the guest of honour as reigning world champion. Carine didn't need to be asked twice and was given permission to go by her parents.

"I'll make sure she meets someone nice," they were assured by Jean-Pierre with a mischievous tone.

The ball was to be held in the Thier-Brau-Hof in Torhout and although I went, I didn't really want to. I really would have preferred to have gone somewhere else with my friend Donald Dewulf and his sister Dorothée, but my father made me go. Jean-Pierre, who had just finished a dance with Carine, spotted me and said to her, "Do you see that boy? Well go and tell him that he's got to have a dance with you. Will you do that for me? He's a good friend of mine and he looks a bit lost."

Carine hesitatingly carried out her orders and, to her great surprise, I accepted her invitation straightaway. Later on in the evening it was my turn to ask her for another dance. This was right at the end of the evening, as we had already put our coats on ready to go back to Jean-Pierre and Annie's house.

"Go ahead Carine, it's all right," Jean-Pierre encouraged her.

"We'll go and wait for you in the car."

A couple of weeks later, Jean-Pierre and I were at the Thier-Brau-Hof again, this time for the presentation of the *Het Volk Trophy*. Guess who he had brought with him again? That's right, Carine. She told me on this occasion that she went to the De Germinal Hall in Izegem every Sunday afternoon with some of her girlfriends.

One day while I was out training with Jean-Pierre, I asked him if he knew where the De Germinal Hall was.

"You can stay at our house on Saturday night," he replied. "I'm kicking off a football match in Roeselare on Sunday afternoon. As soon as I've finished there, we'll go to the hall together in the car."

I sent Carine a letter saying that I would be arriving at about four. Jean-Pierre assured me that the hall wouldn't be opening until seven o'clock in the evening that Sunday.

"That means we've got plenty of time, so we might as well stay at the football match after the kick-off." he announced like a proper comedian.

The story ended with us arriving in Izegem at a quarter to eight and Carine had been waiting for me since four. Another quarter of an hour and she would have had to catch the bus home. Jean-Pierre had worked everything out perfectly again.

At Christmas I was introduced to Carine's parents. My uncle gave me a lift as far as the church in Rumbeke and from there I went looking for the right house number in Blinde Rodenbachstraat on foot. Carine's mother made us some coffee and we had a piece of cake. We all felt rather uncomfortable at this first meeting, with little being said and no-one seeming to dare to speak. Fortunately, Carine's brother soon started a conversation about cycling and Carine's parents listened attentively to what the young man from Lombardsijde had to say for himself.

The first time I introduced Carine to my parents was during my Supporters' Ball in the De Wedergeboorte Hall. My father was very annoyed because I hadn't given him any notice, but by the end of the evening he had cooled down. Carine won my mother's heart from their very first meeting. She had to act diplomatically with my father though, as he feared that she might mean the end of his son's blossoming cycling career. However, thanks to my mother he was quickly won over when he realised that Carine would be able to provide great support for me as my career developed.

From then on, I would see Carine, who continued to work for a glove manufacturer until we got married, twice a week at her house. My father always had to take me to Rumbeke as I still could not drive. At first he would sit in the car while I was with Carine until one day when Carine's mother went out to him and said, "Mr Maertens, why don't you come inside?"

That was when the ice was broken between the two families once and for all.

Not every girl is cut out to become a cyclist's wife, as they have a great deal to put up with. She is the one who has to face her husband when he returns from a race feeling edgy and in a bad mood.

Although there used to be a greater feeling of solidarity among riders' wives, Carine rarely came to races with me and instead she made sure I had a hot meal waiting for me when I arrived home. For me that was more important. A worker never takes his wife to work with him, does he? The very sight of riders' wives showing-off and gossiping makes me shudder. Carine would never do that, even in my glory days. When she did go to races it was to Criteriums in our area because she would see people she knew there.

For the rest of the time she had work enough, not only practical things like washing and ironing my racing kit but also managing for herself when I was riding abroad.

Because they have to spend so much time on their own, riders' wives tend to be independent types. In the light of what we had to go through later, Carine had a lot more to put up with than other cycling wives. Without her I would never have been able to get through everything the way I did, and for that I can count myself lucky.

5 Naive Realism

As a brand new amateur I'd only had two races in my own country behind me when I was called up by national team-manager, Lucien Acou, in March 1971, for the Tour of Algeria. At the time I was doing my military service under Commandant Lierman at the military base in Lombardsijde. After a few months I was transferred, at my own request, to the officer's mess at Middel-kerke, where Commandant Widart was my superior officer. He let me choose my own hours pretty much, and in the afternoons I was usually free to train. When I became Champion of Belgium in Nandrin that year I pulled off a tactical ploy that would guarantee me even more freedom. I invited all the journalists to the mess over the next few days and let Commander Widart stand next to me on the photos; it certainly paid off.

"As the national title-holder you've probably got a lot of work to do, haven't you?" he asked me.

"Yes I have, commander," I answered. "From now on I have to race somewhere nearly every day."

"Oh, just give me a telephone call on the morning of the race. As far as I'm concerned that will do." So from then on my military service became a gentleman's life.

The Tour of Algeria lasted from March 16th to 28th, but the Belgian team stayed there for a couple of weeks beforehand at a training camp. Now and then I would phone my fiancée Carine and my parents in Belgium in the evening. That's how, on the night before the first stage, I found out that Jean-Pierre Monseré had been killed during a race in Retie. This shock news had an enormous impact on me. My first reaction was; 'I'm not starting the race.' Lucien Acou was categorically against this though, and looking back on it he was right: nothing could change what had happened. So I did start, but I could see his face flashing through my mind every day we were in Algeria.

The climate was superb, it wasn't as stiflingly hot as I thought it would be, and we stayed in marvellous hotels with marble everywhere. The food wasn't much to write home about, though. One evening the menu for every team was roast lamb. It was placed in the middle of the table with all the Belgian team sitting round and everyone was allowed to slice off as much as he wanted with his own knife. When we started we could see that the meat hadn't been thoroughly cooked and the blood was dripping on to our hands. My appetite disappeared at once.

As well as the East Germans, French, Swedish and North Africans there were Polish and Russian riders on the Tour as well and it was these two nations who were to dominate proceedings. In some of the stages, however, I did manage a high placing. Our team members were clearly not experienced enough against riders from other countries to be able to lead me out for the sprint in the way that the others could. Not only were our opponents older than us but they knew all sorts of tricks like pushing and pulling; indeed they weren't afraid of *orchestral manoeuvres in the dark*. I found out a lot about sprinting out there, not least the realisation that during the lead-up to a sprint you sometimes have to do some work with your elbows. Up to then I'd never had any cause to be aware of this, but in the light of the more serious examples of it that I came across as a professional, the Tour of Algeria provided an excellent training school.

The leadership the Eastern Bloc counties enjoyed contrasted sharply to ours. Our coach, Lucien Acou, the father-in-law of Eddy Merckx, clearly treated the trip more as a personal outing than as an opportunity to give the riders some overseas experience. People I did have a great deal of respect for, though, were mechanic Theo Mertens and the physio of the national team, both of whom took their jobs seriously. Anyway, it was in Algeria where I learned how to ride a race. In the final overall classification I took third place and that exceeded my greatest expectations. In the end the winner was Krzeszowiec after world champion Szurkowski had been in the lead for much of the tour. Hanusik, one of the few riders with a beard, also made a good impression. 'How is it that there are so few bearded men in the peloton?' is a question I've been asked on more than one occasion. The answer is very simple; not having a beard is more hygienic. Riders generally present a horrible picture after a heavy race, with snot and dribble all over, and that's without a beard, so what do you think it would be like *with* one?

By this time I was already going to see the kinetics-therapist Jacques Delva at Menen four times a week. He had worked with Monseré and had introduced me to Jean-Pierre. On photographs taken during interviews you can often see me sitting in a yoga position on my settee. I learned this form of relaxation from Delva. The logic behind the yoga exercises I did at Delva's is as follows: If you hold a piece of elastic stretched out for a long time and then let go of it, it doesn't go back to its original state completely. The same happens to muscles when they are heavily burdened. Thanks to the yoga movements and the stretching exercises with weights that Jacques devised for me, they were made elastic again. This has played a big part in my physical condition throughout my career.

In order to be considered for the amateur world championships in Mendrisio, by being a member of the national team, I was required by the BWB to take part in a training camp at De Haan on the coast. I didn't want to, or to put it another way, my father didn't want me to. Neither of us saw the point of it. The camp was mainly intended to be preparation for the world championship 100 kilometre time trial and I was under no illusions that attending it would book me a ticket. At the same time, though, if I didn't go to the camp there was the risk that I'd be out of the running for a place in the road race, and so I accepted the invitation. National coach Lucien Acou needed eight riders and he divided them into two teams of four, which he had riding against each other. Neither money nor effort were spared; he had a circuit of about 15kms marked out and a policeman or a marshal was placed at every crossroads. We had to cover the 100kms. of the race each time. The team I was in had to start five minutes before the other one because it wasn't as good. The other foursome, Louis Verreydt, Staf Van Cauter, Ludo Van Der Linden and Staf Hermans eventually became world champions in Mendrisio, a performance that has never been equalled by a team representing Belgium in that discipline since. Two of the four, Louis Verreydt and Ludo Van Der Linden, have died since then, and that cannot be put down to coincidence. It is a fact that the foursome were *prepared* in a special way before that illustrious race. I saw one or two things with my own eyes. The premature deaths of Verreydt and Van Der Linden have their roots in that time at the De Haan training camp, of that I am convinced.

In the Lylita Hotel where we were staying, the owner Henri Bauwens had a monkey in a cage. One day we threw him a pep pill. The monkey sniffed it and then threw it away. After that we tried stuffing the pep pill into a piece of chocolate. It seemed as though the monkey wasn't born yesterday, because it got the pill out of the chocolate and tossed it to the ground again. Our third attempt was successful though. We ground the pill into a powder and mixed it into the foam of a chocolate drink. Suspecting nothing, the monkey swallowed everything. The result was that while receiving encouraging shouts from our side of the bars he became super-active inside his cage. It would seem that it did not suit him 100% and neither did it suit the fishes we gave it to, as they all died of it.

On July 25th in Nandrin I became national champion ahead of Ludo Van Staeyen and Ludo Noels. It was an unbelievably tough championship with only 19 riders reaching the finish. As if it wasn't difficult enough anyway, there was a hailstorm towards the end. I realised fairly quickly that there would be a high number of riders dropping out, so during the first half of the race I made sure I was among those at the front and stayed on the alert, while at the same time making sure I didn't use up too much energy. At the start of the last circuit there were six of us at the front. Because I feared Ludo Van Staeyen's finishing sprint, I attacked on the descent before the Mont Halleux. I started this final climb with a lead of 200 metres and by then it was too late for anyone to threaten my lead.

Winning the Belgian tricolour jersey didn't come as such a surprise for me. I've always been able to *gear myself up* for certain races, and that was how I was at the start of this one, full of self-confidence. Things can of course happen to you that you can do nothing about. A crash right in front of you that you can't avoid can be enough to ruin your whole race. Luckily, in Nandrin that didn't happen and I was able to see the tactics I had used pay off. That morning we had arrived very early in the Walloon village. During the reception in the evening the pastor mentioned in his short speech the fact that he had seen the new champion at his mass that morning.

Two coach-loads of my supporters travelled to Nandrin. My mother wept with joy while Carine stood soberly at a distance, watching what was going on on the podium. The next day I went to lay flowers at the grave of Jean-Pierre Monseré.

As the national title-holder, the BWB obviously couldn't leave me at home for the World Championship road race in Mendrisio. otherwise they probably would have. According to the federation

I had shown signs of disruptive behaviour and had done too much of my own thing in De Haan. That might have been the case but it depends on your point of view. It's true that I didn't stay in the hotel sleeping every evening and sometimes I did some extra training on my own, but I could hardly be blamed for incidents involving someone else. I enjoyed having a glass of wine with a meal but that can be put down partly to the French origins of my mother. Coach Lucien Acou would always be sitting at the table with a full bottle of wine in front of him for himself. One day I grabbed the bottle and poured myself a drink. The other riders gaped in disbelief at this scene, but none of them dared to follow my example. The next day Mr Acou was kind enough to come and fill my glass himself.

Alongside me in the Belgian team for the road race on Saturday 4th September in Mendrisio were the four from the team time trial; Staf Van Cauter, Louis Verreydt, Staf Hermans and Ludo Van Der Linden, plus Marc Demeyer. The Dutchman, Fedor den Hertog, was the first to attack and stayed on the offensive throughout the race. In the final stages he jumped away again and at first only the Frenchman, Marcel Duchemin, was able to stay with him until Ludo Van Der Linden managed to join the two of them. Van Der Linden was something of a favourite of Acou. It was no coincidence when straight after the world championship race he made it known that he was to turn professional with Eddy Merckx's (Acou's son in law) team.

Towards the end of the race, Van Der Linden must have already been thinking the world championship was his, being in the company of two riders not as fast in the sprint as him, but eventually the trio were caught by our group. It was then that he promised me that if he wasn't on his own on the last lap he would lead out the sprint for me. Through my incredible naiveté, I was well and truly stitched up. At a kilometre from the finish line the Russian, Gusiatnikow, made a do-or-die effort. Instead of leading me out, Van Der Linden blocked me off on the left hand side so that I was forced to try the other side. In the meantime, the Pole, Szurkowski, was in full flight, with the Frenchman, Regis Ovion, in an ideal position. It was to be the first in a series of world titles of which I was robbed. Explaining his actions afterwards, Van Der Linden said that he hadn't seen exactly where I was. As if he didn't know which way the wind blew.

There was no point in holding a grudge and I consoled myself with my silver medal. There was a good atmosphere in the Belgian team on the Sunday evening after the world championships for professionals, in which Eddy Merckx had been beaten by Felice Gimondi. After we had eaten our evening meal and were sitting around the swimming pool eating cake while waiting to catch the night train from Lugano to Brussels, someone suddenly had the bright idea of throwing me and the chair on which I was sitting into the water. Because of the amount of chlorine in the pool, my best trousers shrank several inches. To make things worse I had to dive back into the water as I'd lost one of my shoes. Jef Dhont, who had come along as physio for the pro's from the Flandria team, fancied a swim and left his clothes on a chair behind him. Just as he was getting out of the pool he laughingly remarked, "Ha, ha, just look at that, someone's clothes are floating on the water!" When he turned round it became clear to him; they were his.

There was supposed to be a restaurant car on the train but in the event there wasn't and we arrived at Brussels station absolutely famished. Once there though – with me in my shrunken trousers – we were decorated with flowers. As soon as the ceremony had finished, professional rider Eric Leman and I jumped into the train for Ostend where Carine and my father were waiting for me. Leman, Carine and I went straight to the Montgomery tearoom and had waffles with whipped cream and fruit, pancakes and Irish coffees. Eric and I looked sick with hunger and the reason we gorged ourselves with this sort of food was that we hadn't been allowed to eat what we wanted during the build-up to the championships.

A week later, on 12th September, I took my revenge for the defeat in Mendrisio by winning the pre-Olympic road race in Munich against the cream of the amateurs who would be battling for gold the following year in the same city. During the final kilometres, while everyone was looking out for the lightning quick Dutchman, Piet van Katwijk, it was me that shot away like a rocket. Only Joergen Emil Hansen could get on to my trail, but I made a long straight sprint keeping the Dane ten seconds behind me.

In October I heard that I had been selected for the Olympic Games in 1972. The condition was that I took part in the preparation programme the Federation had set out. Included in it were the Tour of Algeria, the Tour of Morocco and two training camps. I refused to let myself be put through all of this again, not least because my father was completely against it. He thought it was a stupid idea. Behind this opposition lay the continuing conflict between my father and coach Acou. The two of them were never on the same wavelength. My father was of the opinion that we had always been able to find races in Belgium which were tough enough, and if we continued to do so the BWB's schedule would be unnecessary. Supporters obviously like to see their favourite racing in their own area, yet the rider doesn't get anything out of it. My cycling was my father's concern and that took precedence over everything else. You need supporters but you should not let them decide for you how you carry out your career.

Our determined stance didn't go down well with the gentlemen at the BWB and my name was struck off the list of pre-selected riders for Munich. My performances during 1972, however, gave them no option but to pick me again.

6 Black September.

The fact that I no longer belonged to the hardcore squad for Munich didn't give me a moment's concern. For me personally it was as clear as day that I would eventually be selected for the Olympic Games, they just couldn't go without me. It was almost comparable to the situation which occurred in the 1987-88 cyclo-cross season concerning Roland Liboton. The BWB threatened all winter to leave him at home for the world championship, but when it came down to it they gladly took him to Switzerland because they realised they would have been cutting off their nose to spite their face if they hadn't selected him. Oh, how the decision makers of the BWB just love to demonstrate their power, and on that score nothing has changed in more than 15 years.

I won one race after another from the start of 1972, including the important season's opener, Het Volk (Ghent-Ghent). My tally for the season would eventually reach 30 victories, a total approached by no other Belgian amateur that year. What I predicted would happen took place in May when I was once again chosen for the Olympic squad.

On 9th July I added the West Flemish Championship at Bavikhove to my list of honours when I beat Rino Vandromme, the rider who had made my life a misery in the newcomer and junior categories. On becoming an amateur Vandromme had joined WSC Torhout, the club of which I had been a member for several years, but this did nothing to improve our relationship. In the Grand-Prix Karel Van Wijnendaele, for example, six riders were at the front, including Vandromme and me. It had been agreed by the club leaders beforehand that if he was with me in a good breakaway, I was to lead him out for the sprint. Part of the circuit was made up of narrow, twisting lanes and at a certain point I attacked and the only one who was able to go with me was Vandromme. I had already seen my father clearly shaking his head and this made it clear to me that I should go for the win myself. On the last circuit I was worrying myself stupid about how I should go about shaking off Vandromme, especially since he had never gone to the front. My solution to the problem was rather unusual, I rode straight ahead onto a path instead of taking a bend to the left. Vandromme, who had been protecting himself from the wind by being right behind me, could do nothing else but follow me onto the path.

"What the hell are you doing?" he shouted. The time it took for us to get back on to the main road allowed the others to catch us up. A little further on and I attacked again, this time managing to stay out on my own. I won, but neither Vandromme nor the club leaders of WSC Torhout were very pleased about it.

I couldn't take part in the national championships that year as two days before the event I had been knocked down by a lorry during a training ride and ended up under a tram which left me with a fractured skull. In August, however, I had recovered sufficiently to be able to set off with the rest of the Olympic selections to the William Tell Tour in Switzerland.

For the Olympic Games in Munich Ludo Delcroix took the place of Ludo Van Der Linden in the foursome that had won the 100 kilometre team time trial in Mendrisio a year earlier. The four who were to take part in the road race were national champion, Lucien De Brauwere, Frans Van Looy, Staf Hermans and me. Originally the road race had been planned for Wednesday, 6th September, but because of the chaos following the activities of the Black September terrorist group in the Olympic Village the evening before, the event was put back for one day. On that fateful Tuesday evening we witnessed the actions of Black September at first hand as the building where the Israeli athletes were taken was right across the road from ours. We could see black hoods, white jackets and machine-guns being fired at random and had to draw the curtains to our rooms to make sure the terrorists didn't aim their weapons at us.

This tragic incident ruined our concentration completely. Up to then the preparations in Munich, where we had been for two weeks, had been going very well. With me were my father, the kinetics therapist, Jacques Delva and Julien Devriese, behind whose derny I had trained on the route. Once again this was to the consternation of coach Lucien Acou who accused me of taking the preparations too personally, thereby having a negative influence on the rest of the team. That was nonsense though, and I had an excellent relationship with the other riders, It was just that Acou was rarely around to notice it. The number of times we got lost in Munich and were only able to get back by employing some detective work was too great for me to remember. Then, before the start, he declared that he was worried that maybe we had all trained a bit too much. I wonder how he could have known in view of the fact that whenever you needed him the first place you tried was Fräulein Watrau's café.

In the Olympic race I finished 13th. The Dutch gave the opposition a lesson in team discipline that day and held the rest of us in a vice. When Hennie Kuiper escaped, I tried to get a reaction going, but with Cees Priem and Fedor Den Hertog as loyal watchdogs always on my trail, it was doomed to failure.

7   The Step-Up.

The Olympic road race in Munich was to be my last important one
as an amateur. Although I deliberately waited to see how it would
go – a medal would have upped my value – for some time it had
already been settled that I was to become a professional in Briek
Schotte's Flandria team, and nowhere else. In fact I was receiving
a monthly wage of BF 40,000 throughout my second season as an
amateur from Flandria. That sort of thing happens. The Italian
kitchen giant, Scic, also offered me the chance to turn
professional. Team manager Carlo Chiappano, together with the
cycle manufacturer Ernesto Colnago, personally came to my
parents' house for that reason. On hearing about this, Paul Claeys
the director of the bike manufacturer Flandria in Zedelgem,
asked me to sign a provisional contract worth BF 40,000 a month.

When I stepped up to the ranks of the professionals I was
forbidden by Claeys to stipulate the exact amount on my contract.
Directeur sportif Briek Schotte was the third person present
during that conversation.

"Well Freddy, how much do you think you're worth?" asked
Paul Claeys from behind his desk.

"Oh, I don't really know," I answered. "That's for you to
decide, isn't it?"

Paul Claeys started doing some sums on his calculator with
Briek Schotte standing behind him. When Briek saw the final
figure appear he shouted out in a startled way, "But *Mr Pol*,
you're not going to give him that much are you?"

"Briek, it's got nothing to do with you," I replied. "This is
between me and Paul Claeys."

The monthly wage was set at BF 90,000 and Briek thought it
was too much. What right did he have, though? After all is said
and done, he was only an employee like me.

The day I decided to take the step up to the professionals, I was
still only 21, and therefore I had to make a special application to
the BWB but this was only a formality really. First of all though, I
helped WSC Torhout to victory in the national inter-club team
time trial in Tournai. Of the four riders who started in each team
it was the time of the third rider that counted for the end result. Of
our foursome Jacques Gryspeerdt had to drop back fairly soon

and Rino Vandromme was hardly able to take over at the front, so it was left to Michel Pollentier and me to do the job ourselves that day.

On the Wednesday evening before Paris-Tours, I received the official sanction to switch to the professionals straightaway. The next day I took part in my very last amateur race in Tielt. On the Friday I did an 80 kilometre training stint with Walter Godefroot, one of the old campaigners at Flandria. At that point in time I could have had no idea that during the course of my career he was to have it in for me on more than one occasion, for instance during the first time I rode a six day race with him. It was originally planned that he would be paired with Robert Van Lancker, an excellent track cyclist in Grenoble. Godefroot, however, was happy to form a duo with me.

"I'll do it as an act of friendship for you, Freddy," he said. "I'd be glad to teach you how best to ride the track."

Afterwards, I found out that he had got the manager to knock BF 150,000 from my contract for the event. A very nice *act of friendship* that was, wasn't it?

In Paris-Tours, the classic in which I had made my debut among the *big boys* on October 1st, I finished 26th. I noticed straightaway that things were done differently than with the amateurs, with team tactics playing a major role. Taking my place in the professional peloton at the end of the season was somewhat misleading, in that many riders were already tired of racing, while I was really keen. That meant that I often didn't judge riders at their true worth and I sometimes gambled on the wrong horse. Those who I thought I had to keep an eye on didn't do anything. As it happened the winner of Paris-Tours that year was a total outsider, Noel Vantyghem, who like me, had once won the Criterium of the Westhoek.

The following day I came 7th in Oostrozebeke, the day after 4th in Templeuve and on 5th October I gained my first professional victory in the 'kermesse' race at Zwevezele. Obviously I realise that kermesses have a poor reputation and it is thought that everything has been *arranged* beforehand. Each kermesse is different though, and in Zwevezele, Christian Callens and I sprinted for all we were worth. At first Marcel Omloop was with us but because of the rapid speed he was dropped, leaving a sprint between the two of us in the end.

I'd be the first to admit that at kermesses I've sometimes paid riders who were with me in the leading group to do their share of the work so that we would stay out of reach of the chasers. I don't call that *bribery* though, but simply asking for the help of riders who knew they wouldn't win. At Flandria we rode plenty of kermesses and later, when I was team leader, it was a principle of mine to let a team-mate win as often as possible.

One day we set off for a kermesse at Adinkerke. The team trained over 120 kilometres that morning. There was a biting northerly wind and we got ourselves into the front row and went hell for leather from the off. The outcome was a quick escape of 8 riders with 6 of them from Flandria. Roger Verschaeve hadn't won all season so I said to him, "Attack, Roger. Today it's your turn."

What was so wrong in denying Verschaeve, who'd ridden himself into the ground for me all season, that bit of pleasure. The BWB representative in the following car, André Commeyne (later to become the chairman of the West Flemish section and one of the few figures in the Federation for whom I have any respect) thought differently about it. He drove alongside me and accused me of not attempting to win myself and my reaction was to climb off there and then. Later I had to pay a fine of BF 5,000.

In those days I didn't like kermesses at all – always the same circuit and so monotonous. However, because our sponsors wanted it, we always had to take part. In 1975 for example, I won Paris-Brussels and was expected to be at the start in Zwevegem the following day.

"The organisers are good people," was how Briek would silence any rumblings of discontent in those days.

Well yes, there are a lot of *good people* in the world. But whether you'd win a war with them on your side is another matter.

The man in the street tends to associate kermesses with words such as *payments* and *deals*. In this, exaggeration knows no bounds. Anyone who thinks he can win a race will have a go, but if he's not sure about it, he pays out to make sure. That's the way it is. On our licenses it says we are *professional* riders. If you think you're not going to win, you'd be a fool to say: "I don't need the money." If you lose, how would you rather go home in the evening to your wife and child: with or without a bit of extra cash?

With Flandria we didn't need to put the money up front very often. That is because we had such a solid team that we could usually control a kermesse race, and we didn't have to worry about any intruders. The only thing we once did was to let someone from another team win a 'prime,' purely out of embarrassment.

I regard it as a positive step that in Belgium kermesses have been replaced by the so-called *regional races*, of which there is a maximum of one organised per day. The fact that directeurs sportifs can also follow in their own cars is also good because it keeps them at loggerheads with each other more than ever before. Forget any ideas about deals being made between them. I'm not saying it doesn't happen, but it is certainly less than one might suppose, because the sponsor demands victories. A good deal between directeurs sportifs would be if they agree not to knock each other into a ditch. I often hear people claim: "It's *only* a kermesse." Well, I'd just like to see them try to ride a few circuits.

Nowadays, bookmakers are not allowed to stand alongside the circuit with their boards showing the odds. I found their disappearance sad because I always felt that their presence helped to create a certain ambience. They were accused of having too much influence on the outcome of a race, but when Michel Pollentier, Marc Demeyer and I were together at Flandria, it never made any difference to us what they were hoping to see happen. It was just the opposite in fact and we often used to lead them a merry dance. For example, in 1974 and 1976 I won the Championship of Flanders in Koolskamp, a race that was (and still is) generally regarded as being completely manipulated by the bookies. In fact, the second time I won I wasn't even supposed to join in the sprint, but Marc Demeyer egged me on to have a go. In the final bend before the finish Walter Planckaert blocked me so it was obvious that he was *in the pocket* of Frans Verbeek, who I ended up beating in the sprint. I had even been given a bidon with a ticket in it, on which was the name of the rider who was supposed to win and how much I would get in return.

So you see, the bookmakers didn't always have it their own way. In the end it was the riders who made the decisions.

8 Smart Businessmen in Barcelona

When I started my first full season as a professional in 1973, I looked on it as being a learning experience. While Walter Godefroot remained the main star in the team, I wanted to discover how much I was worth. Therefore I put myself in the service of Godefroot and put any ambitions of forcing myself up to the position of team leader to the back of my mind. In any case, Briek Schotte never really believed in a team having one absolute leader. That was one of the main reasons why he was replaced as directeur sportif by Guillaume Driessens at the end of 1975.

Before each classic Briek would say: "We'll have to get together to discuss our tactics."

On the eve of the race the whole team would sit together at a table, usually just before a meal, to deliberate. Briek would say indecisively: "How are we going to go about it tomorrow? Fred's riding well, and Michel's riding well, and . . ."

When it came to the crunch, we always seemed to be ten riders who were all going well at the moment, according to Briek. Who was going to wait for whom? Who would give a wheel to whom? We once had a taster of that, thanks to Briek, during an edition of Paris-Roubaix. I had a flat tyre and although Paul Verschuere saw me standing at the side of the road, he rode straight past me. The explanation I was given was quite simple. Paul had the right physique to ride well over the cobbles and he'd heard the previous evening that we were to set out with ten leaders, so he thought he didn't have to look out for me. He left me there standing like an idiot.

Without fail, Briek would say: "We shall wait and see how things turn out during the race." This policy seemed all wrong to me and it made the tactical discussions totally pointless.

The theory supported by Briek was the exact opposite to the Merckx doctrine in which all the other riders understood that they must sacrifice themselves for the one leader. I take my hat off to Briek Schotte's performances as a rider, but I would question his abilities as a directeur sportif. He let everyone do as they wished. The only thing that mattered to him was that one of the team won and that he could make money, ours by rights, for Paul Claeys. Suppose the team received BF 25,000 for appearing at a kermesse, Briek would share it out as follows: "5,000 for Maertens, 5,000 for Demeyer and 5,000 for Pollentier." The rest would then go to Paul Claeys. What did the organisers do, though, when a big name rider took part in a race for BF 5,000? They laughed into their beer, that's what they did, because they knew only too well that other organisers would have to pay BF 80,000 to get you to start. No wonder these others felt cheated. News like that spreads very quickly, even though they were all *good people.*

A further illustration of the above point was that as another consequence of Briek's unorthodox method of reckoning I still had to pay tax on the BF 15,000 that was really meant for me, even though BF 5,000 of it had gone to Demeyer and BF 5,000 had gone to Pollentier. The same thing almost happened to me when I won the Super Prestige Trophy for the first time in 1976, this time with Lomme Driessens as boss. A prize of BF 350,000 went with it and as always I divided the prize money into three, but made sure Marc and Michel both signed a receipt to say they had received their share.

As I've already said, the 1973 season was one in which I was out to gain as much experience as possible. I never thought of myself as *the new Merckx*, it was journalists who continually used that phrase. I knew only too well that after a tough series of spring classics I was never going to win the Tour de France. That was crystal clear to me from the first season.

In 1973 I was only 21 and knew that I would have to use my strength sparingly. I wanted to grow as a rider and was convinced that by being careful to do so I would be able to attain higher standards. Even Eddy Merckx kept very distant from me during that first year. Despite everything that later went on between us I'm still openly prepared to say that he is the best rider I have ever raced against. Whenever I could beat him I did and beating the *very best* gave me the greatest satisfaction. As a newcomer I couldn't count on any favours from the established riders, and that was exactly how I wanted it to be. More than that though, I regarded it as a very positive thing for a promising young rider to have to battle against the experienced men. It is both stimulating and character-building. It's difficult for me to say what Roger De Vlaeminck thought of me in the early days, simply because you never knew where you stood with him. He would wait to see which way the wind was blowing and would sometimes form a coalition with Merckx against me and sometimes with others against Merckx. I couldn't make head nor tail of it. One thing is certain, you could count on Eric De Vlaeminck a great deal more than you could Roger.

In the classics I finished in the leading places several times: 2nd in the Tour of Flanders, 5th in Ghent-Wevelgem, 8th in the Amstel Gold Race, 5th in Paris-Roubaix, 3rd in the Henninger Turm (Frankfurt) and 8th in the national championship at Soumagne. I wouldn't go as far as saying that if someone other than Briek Schotte had been my directeur sportif, I would have definitely won a classic. That would be an easy excuse. Or would it? Maybe I would have done better than my second place in the Tour of Flanders if that had been the case. There were four of us at the front, Eddy Merckx, Eric Leman, Willy De Geest and me. De Geest was then riding for Rokado, the team managed by Lomme Driessens. Driessens would rather have seen anyone other than Merckx win, so he gave instructions to De Geest – who didn't stand a chance of winning himself – to lead out the sprint for me. Schotte wouldn't have any of this, though. Merckx then took over the role of pacemaker for Leman, as he would rather have seen an old fox win the best of the Flemish classics for the third time than see the new boy, Maertens, win it for the first time.

My most satisfying triumph in 1973 was the Four Days of Dunkirk and the final time trial in particular. It was a personal test which I passed using a 54x13 gear. Among those I beat were Joop Zoetemelk, Raymond Poulidor and Frans Verbeeck. I had never dared to dream of winning it, although I thought I would manage a place in the first three. The reason that win gave me so much satisfaction is that you have to view time-trialling as a key discipline in cycling. It can be compared to the place poetry has within literature.

Time-trialling: *the most individual expression of the most individual performance.*

I was selected for the team for the world championships at the Montjuich circuit in Barcelona, my first as a professional. When I look back on what happened, although I wouldn't say it was the greatest disappointment of my career I would definitely say it deserves the title of *the most sordid machination* ever practised on me.

What exactly is the truth behind the famous Barcelona row? At the heart of it lies the commercial power struggle between two rival cycle component manufacturers. On the one side was the established Italian make, Campagnolo, and on the other was the Japanese firm, Shimano, which was trying to win a slice of the European market. During a training ride with the Belgian team on the circuit a car pulled up alongside us and sitting in it was the head of Campagnolo.

I heard him say to Walter Godefroot from the car, in Italian: *"At all costs Shimano must not win on Sunday."*

I didn't know what all of this meant. That year Shimano were the co-sponsors of our team, Flandria, so like me Walter rode a Shimano-equipped bike. It became clear to me afterwards that Campagnolo had paid off Godefroot, one of the key figures in the Belgian camp.

I swear that conversation took place. During the following night I lay awake for a long time going over in my head what I'd heard. When the following morning I told my employer Paul Claeys who was in Barcelona with us, his answer was: "Oh, there's no need to go looking for things behind what is really there. Just carry on believing in yourself."

On the Saturday evening, during a meeting of the Belgian squad, Merckx offered BF 100,000 to any of his compatriots who would ride for him. De Vlaeminck and I refused and said we would be riding for ourselves. Godefroot didn't reject Merckx's offer out of hand, and with that you could see the double dealing which he would not allow to be seen openly.

We reached the final stages with four riders at the front: Eddy Merckx and Felice Gimondi (both on Campagnolo-equipped bikes), Luis Ocana (on a Zeus-equipped bike) and me (on a Shimano-equipped bike). With three circuits to go Merckx attacked – which was no coincidence as it happened shortly after I'd asked him to take it easy as I was struggling with cramp at that point. Not that it was too bad. I would still be able to lead out the sprint for him, as I had promised during the race.

There was no co-operation at all between the Italian, Gimondi, and the Spaniard, Ocana, who had won the Tour de France that season. As Merckx escaped I was thinking that if I went as well, Ocana wouldn't close the gap for Gimondi and it would have been just as unlikely that Gimondi would follow Merckx since they were both riding with Campagnolo equipment.

My plan worked and during the climb of Montjuich itself I managed to get up to Merckx on my own and took over immediately. However, to my absolute astonishment he refused to do any lead work.

"Come on Eddy, let's get going!" I shouted to him. "You can win, I'll be quite happy with second place." He just carried on, though, and allowed Gimondi and Ocana to come back up to us.

If Merckx and I had pooled our strength, we would have easily been able to stay out of reach. Afterwards some people blamed me for catching up to him, but why shouldn't I have done? I didn't do anything wrong. I didn't bring the other two with me on my wheel, just the opposite in fact. As soon as I was up to Merckx he could have made use of my help and, as it was to turn out, he could have really used it. The simple fact that I was able to close the gap so easily is a clear illustration of the fact that he wasn't on quite such *top form* in Barcelona as he was on many other days.

The moment I got up to him my only thoughts were, 'wouldn't it be great if two Belgians crossed the line first and second.' I know my opponents could argue that I could just as easily have come second by winning the sprint with the following riders and of course they're right. However, on that day I would have loved to have been *His Most Highness's* deputy as he made his triumphal entry. I didn't want to jeopardise his chances of winning, it's just that it would have given me enormous personal satisfaction. I didn't for one second think about the way Benoni Beheydt 'stitched up' Rik Van Looy during the 1963 World Championship in Ronse, with a view to doing the same to *King* Merckx. I was too young for anything like that. Imagine how the Belgian people would have reacted to it. If I had wanted to see serious doubts cast on the healthy progress of my future cycling career, all it would have needed was for me to do such a thing.

When the four of us were back in a group, the understanding still held that I was to lead out the sprint for Merckx. Whether this was a favour to Campagnolo or not I had given him my word and was going to stick to it. What had actually happened, although Merckx never told me, was that he had blown up. Why didn't he say anything so that I could ride my own race? Think of how much credit he would have received from everyone if I had been able to say after the race: "Eddy was really honest and helped a young rider like me become the world champion?"

It was not to be, however, and he remained silent. Like a stupid little fool, I started the sprint from a long way out. Just like he'd asked me to, from a long way out. Why from a long way out? It's obvious now, I was supposed to blow up. Merckx got on to my wheel. I was looking out, waiting, wondering where he'd gone to, still waiting, but he didn't come. Then Gimondi suddenly shot past. Only then did I realise that I had been *knifed in the back* by Merckx and that because his own chance had gone he would have rather seen the Italian win on a Campagnolo-equipped bike than me. I tried to get back up to Gimondi again but he went way off line and nearly knocked me into the fence. Nevertheless he still only managed to beat me by the narrowest of margins. The BWB didn't dare to make a complaint to the race jury because, as Frans Ceulaers, chairman of the national sport commission put it: *"Our colleagues at the Italian Federation are our best friends."*

Once over the finishing line and seething with anger, I shouted to Merckx: "Coward!"

Like an innocent choirboy he began to cry.

After the dope control he got back to our hotel, the El Rancho, before me. He immediately retired to his room with his wife Claudine. When I got back to the hotel, the other Belgian riders were looking at me as if I was a fish out of water, as though I had messed everything up for them. The reason for that, of course, being the BF 100,000 they had been promised if Merckx had become the world champion.

I went to a restaurant with Frans Verbeeck and Herman Van Springel and there I calmly told them my version of events over a meal. When we returned to the hotel we saw Rik Van Linden and a couple of other riders.

"How are we going to sort out the money?" Walter Godefroot asked.

"Yeah, how are we going to sort it out?" I said, repeating his question. "You can't expect me to pay out anything, seeing as I didn't win."

A discussion developed in which all the others, who had gradually trickled in, had their say. There was only one who didn't show up, Merckx. Finally Van Springel and Van Linden made their way with me to his room and demanded that he should tell the entire Belgian team exactly what had happened. Only then did he come down with us, and in front of everyone he admitted that he had indeed *tricked* me. When he let that be known, everybody went mad and he was called everything under the sun. The El Rancho was the scene of one almighty row that night.

Merckx had little alternative but to tell the truth, it was so glaringly obvious. Even Willem Van Wijnendaele, whom you wouldn't exactly call anti-Merckx, wrote in the newspaper *Het Nieuwsblad* the following day:

"So in the end it came down to a sprint for four. Freddy Maertens led Merckx out from a long way, full of authority, and as his helper he was in an ideal position. We also thought that Eddy would launch himself two hundred metres from the line and win easily, but he could hardly get past the man from Lombardsijde. It was Gimondi who, right around the outside, shot forward like an arrow and accelerated past Maertens. Would Freddy have won if the roles had been reversed and he'd have sat in Merckx's position? We definitely think so."

No matter what the average cycling fan may think about it all today, it is an irrefutable fact that Campagnolo had laid out tens of millions of Belgian francs for the world title. Each member of the Italian team received his share, Gimondi got an even bigger lump sum and of course Merckx also made a tidy amount. If the rainbow jersey had ended up on my back it would have been me, thanks to Shimano, who would have become a millionaire in one go.

Two days after the world championships in Barcelona, the spectators at the Criterium in Brasschaat had laid on a smashing reception for me. I even got the impression that I was regarded as a bit of a hero, which made me believe that the man on the street had worked out what had happened. However, misfortune decreed that I would have a heavy fall in the race the 'Acht van Brasschaat.' My right arm had to be set in plaster and this was really annoying for me as it meant that I couldn't take revenge in the Autumn classics for the wrong that I had suffered. As I was now unable to appear in any races it meant that I never saw any journalists, while Merckx was free to convince them that he was right.

I have always been obliged to talk to journalists for the benefit of my sponsors. Nevertheless despite all my contacts with these gentlemen, it hasn't stopped me having a very low opinion of them. Really they are a necessary evil and so it is not worth giving special attention to any single reporter in this book, with the exception of one, André Blancke of *Het Volk,* as he is probably the only journalist with whom I've never had a negative experience.

My criticism of Merckx which appeared in the press after Barcelona rebounded badly back onto me. Since Merckx was thought of as a monument, people felt he could not be touched. I was to touch the monument very often, though. What's more, no matter whose side one chose the rivalry between us both was good for the sport. Organisers played us off against each other on their posters and that would draw in the crowds. For example, the evening criterium at Moorslede in 1976 pulled in 30,000 people. Earlier that day I had ridden a race at Gippingen in Switzerland. A helicopter was waiting at the finishing line to take me immediately to the airfield at Zurich where a private jet was also waiting for me. While the plane, which was to land at Wevelgem, was in the air I had a wash, changed and had something to eat. Once at Wevelgem, I jumped into a motor-cycle sidecar while the rider rode hell-for-leather to Moorslede, and there a mechanic had a bike prepared for me. As I had arrived half an hour later than planned the organiser had inserted a short time trial into the programme for the benefit of the crowd. Merckx was furious. I must say, secretly I rather enjoyed knowing he was suffering and to make matters worse, I won the race.

Despite the Barcelona affair and its aftermath, there was a great ending to the 1973 season. On 10th November Carine and I were married. I was only 21 and she was 18 but we lived a long way from each other and for someone in my position, living for his work, all the travelling to and fro was inconvenient. In terms of the way I wanted to see my career develop, it was better to be married. My father had always said: "Wait until after your first season as a professional because then you'll know how good you are and how much you can earn. If you want to make a living from cycling Carine shouldn't have to go out and work for you, you're supposed to go out and work for her. She needs to be there always to support you."

And that's how it happened. From the first day we lived together Carine gave up working at the glove factory.

After the wedding service there was a reception at Sint-Michiel's Hall in Roeselare, mainly for guests from the cycling world. After that, together with the whole family we were taken to the YMCA in Lombardsijde for the real party. The chef, Rik Ferket, had prepared the menu for the afternoon and there was a running buffet for all the other guests in the evening. All the ingredients for the cold buffet were laid out in a U-shape in which a cycle covered in aluminium foil formed the centrepiece. It was marvellous. Later on in the evening after everyone had eaten I did a lap of honour over the tables for a bit of fun.

Carine and I were exhausted and while most of the guests were still dancing and having fun at 3 o'clock in the morning we were taken back to our house in Gistelstraat, Lombardsijde in the car of my friend Patrick Thomas (whom we called Sis). There the three of us quietly drank a bottle of champagne that I had been keeping in the fridge, and then we went to bed – without Sis.

We didn't go on a honeymoon. Right up to my wedding day I had given my earnings to my parents, something that I never thought of as being unusual. The furniture for our bedroom was bought by my parents, for our dining room by Carine's parents and for our living room by André Ollevier, director of the firm Confortluxe, who were to become our team's co-sponsors the following year with Flandria. During the wedding party we received many presents as well as BF 14,000 in cash. That money was our only starting capital. As I would still have to wait quite a while for my first month's wages of the new season, I was glad to be able to ride some track meetings during the winter. I can still remember the very first meeting. I received BF 15,000 for it and when we got home Carine and I leapt into the air. We must have counted that money out ten times.

9   The hypocritical list

I started the 1974 season in convincing style. On 20th January I was 11th out of 49 starters in a cyclo-cross meeting at Volkegem in which all the top riders took part – not a bad result for a road racer. Although I wasn't bad at cyclo-cross in those days, I was never really very keen on it and I very rarely took part in meetings. The reason I started in Volkegem was that Firmin Van Kerrebroeck, then the national cyclo-cross coach, had expressly asked me to. Michel Pollentier, who had ridden by my side throughout the race, finished one place behind me. Roger De Vlaeminck was the winner that day and Michel and I had bet him three bottles of champagne that he wouldn't lap us, as he predicted. He didn't manage it. The good result Michel and I achieved in Volkegem can be put down to the training both of us had done in the dunes during the winter. We would keep a murderous pace going while training and a lot of people laughed at the vigorous way we would tackle the course we had designed for ourselves. Sometimes other riders would train with us, but we preferred it when it was just the two of us, because the actual purpose of our stints was to go as hard as you could to break the other one. Michel appeared regularly at cyclo-cross events, while I only took part on special occasions like the cyclo-cross pairs event in which I was teamed up with the Dutch television presenter, Barend Servet.

In the Tour of Andalusia everything clicked into place straight-away. Not only did I win overall but I took 7 stages. The reason I was in top form so soon was the result of how I'd spent the winter. A rider gets out of a season what he has put in the previous winter. If he lives like a lord in France and only starts thinking about his bike on New Year's Day, he has already fallen far enough behind to make it difficult for him to catch up again. I always started my preparation for the following season as early as November. I am not exaggerating when I say that with Michel Pollentier I would ride 10,000 kilometres in winter, before we had started a race. I know because Michel kept a detailed record of it all in a book.

In return for the help Walter Godefroot had given me in the Tour of Andalusia – he had set me up beautifully a few times for victories in the sprints – I wanted to help him win one of the classics. In the Flèche Wallonne I rode at the front with Franco Bitossi right up to the one kilometre flag. When I looked round I could see that the group was hot on our heels and Walter was in a great position, so I stayed on Bitossi's wheel and didn't take over the lead again. The bunch shot past us but Frans Verbeeck and Roger De Vlaeminck were quicker than Godefroot. Three weeks later our tactics paid off and Walter won the Henninger Turm in Frankfurt. Despite all this though, Walter and I were gradually growing apart. He belonged to the Merckx generation and could see that I was beginning to believe more and more in my potential to become team leader. The realisation that from now on he would have to watch out for me in his own team led to a few serious confrontations. It was hardly unexpected that the older riders would try to block the rise of young ones like Raas, Knetemann and myself. Even Merckx and De Vlaeminck would team up together for that purpose, but as soon as it went back to everyone for themselves they were deadly rivals again.

1974 was the first full year that Michel Pollentier, Marc Demeyer and I all wore the colours of Flandria together, as Michel had only turned professional in May 1973. I wanted him to go with me when I went pro in October 1972, but Briek Schotte thought that he wasn't talented enough at that time. I thought he was, of course. I had ridden with Michel in our amateur days and was well aware of the bursts of power of which he was capable. Marc Demeyer, on the other hand, was already a professional when I made the switch. The three of us formed a tight trio for several years and we were to have an impact on every major race.

Marc was known as the locomotive of the peloton, a solid block of power. He was robustly built and came over as perhaps rather forceful, although in reality he was the sort of bloke with a big mouth and a small heart. One day we had been racing in Brittany and the next day we were due to appear at the start somewhere else, so Marc – who was having marriage problems at the time – stayed with us that evening. Carine had prepared a delicious cold buffet for our return home.

"Well, just look at that," said Marc. "You've made that specially for me."

"Oh no," said Carine, playing down her work. "I do the same when Freddy's on his own."

Then Marc began to cry. That was a glimpse of the Demeyer

that the outside world didn't know.

It needs to be said that Briek Schotte always had a lot of time for Marc Demeyer, who was his favourite. It probably had something to do with the fact that Briek and Marc came from the same part of the country and also because Marc had been with Flandria longer than Pollentier and me. In 1974 he triumphed in Paris-Brussels after dominating the final stages, while I was busy blocking counter attacks further back. There was always an excellent understanding between Marc, Michel and myself and when one of the three of us won the other two were given an equal share of the winnings.

As far as I was concerned personally, I had to settle once again for high placings that season: 9th in Milan-San Remo, 6th in Ghent-Wevelgem, 7th in Paris-Roubaix, 6th in the Flèche Wallonne, 9th in Liège-Bastogne-Liège and 5th in Tours-Versailles.

During that period there was always a commotion when a product that until then had been allowed, suddenly turned up on the list of banned substances. Many riders, among whom were several well known names, got into trouble: Walter Godefroot in the Flèche Wallonne, Ronald De Witte in Liège-Bastogne-Liège and Joseph Bruyère, Eric Leman and myself in the Tour of Belgium. I was given one month's conditional suspension and my victory in the Tour of Belgium was taken away from me through the addition of a ten minute time penalty. Roger Swerts, who finished second, was thus given the victory as a present. The same thing had happened to him a couple of years earlier in Ghent-Wevelgem when Frans Verbeeck hindered the Italian, Felice Gimondi, in the sprint and was disqualified afterwards.

Why were there, all of a sudden, so many positive doping cases in the spring of 1974? The following is an explanation for it. When a doctor discovered a new product in a urine sample in Italy, all the teams were informed about it. A rider who carried on using it knew that he was making a mistake. In Belgium, however, they did things rather differently. They would keep quiet about a new discovery, let the riders carry on racing, and then out of the blue they would issue a list of the names of the riders who had been found using it. To me, that is typical of the BWB who have never failed to do things in a completely underhand way.

It was Professor Debackere of the veterinary section of the University of Ghent who carried out the tests on Rilatine, the product in question. I have always thought of it as symbolic that as a cyclist, my urine was tested there of all places. In spite of that and the strict standards Professor Debackere maintains I still regard him as a person of integrity. In the chapter which covers the year 1985 it will become obvious why. The BWB seemingly found him to be too full of integrity since in the last few years Ernest De Vuyst, the present chairman of the national sport committee, has only wanted to use the labs of Professor Heyndrickx for drug testing. At the same time, though, the Ministry of Public Health still has every faith in Professor Debackere.

Riders who have been found positive usually make the excuse that it was an effect of the cough syrup they had been using. That isn't always as lame an excuse as it may sound. It might well be true if Ephedrine is involved, although of course it is naive to believe that all positive cases are a consequence of taking cough syrup. One of the problems for a rider is that often he is not allowed to take the medicine which would best fight his particular complaint. Why does somebody take cough syrup? To get rid of a cough. If a rider is prescribed it by his doctor he has nothing to worry about. However he must not take on the role of a chemist himself, he hasn't the training to do that. As a layman, just try to decipher the formula for one of these products.

"They take everything," the public say. *"Even ones like De Vlaeminck who have never been caught,"* If you are taking strange things every day, of course you'll never finish the Tour de France. But anyone who says they can do it *naturally* is a liar. You have to be medically treated so that you don't do anything stupid off your own back. It is also true that drugs are partly a psychological matter, and in this context every cyclist is rather like a small child. One complaint that is generally directed at sportsmen is that everything, including their health, is geared up for a short career. Even during the euphoric times success brought me, however, I thought about the future. Why else would I have gone to my doctor every ten days for a medical examination? Because it was necessary and because it was part and parcel of my profession. As soon as anything went wrong with my health I wanted to know exactly what was the matter. When I retired I allowed myself to

be thoroughly examined. It gave me great peace of mind to know that all my delicate organs – my kidneys, adrenal glands and hormone levels – were functioning normally.

The list of banned products in cycling is hypocritical in two ways. In the first place there are products on the list that are much less harmful than others that aren't on it, and in the second place, why is a certain product on the banned list in one country but not in another? It is all so confusing that it must inevitably lead to misery. Let me just repeat my accusation about what happened in 1974 again. Why were the teams in Italy warned while those in Belgium weren't? That year's drug affair can best be compared to a hypothetical situation in which the police suddenly reduce the maximum speed in a built up area from 60kph to 50kph without letting anybody know. Should that happen it would be inevitable that a deluge of fines and warnings would follow.

Furthermore, from a rider's viewpoint, there is little point in requesting a second opinion. At dope controls, as is generally known, the person being tested has to pass urine into two bottles that are both immediately sealed up. Can you honestly expect an eminent physician to change his decision on the strength of a second opinion on the other bottle? No, of course not. To me, it would seem more sensible if the rider could take the second sealed bottle home with him so that, in case of appeal, the contents of it could be examined in another laboratory.

Briek Schotte wanted me to ride in the 1974 Tour de France, but I decided it was still too early for that. I didn't feel quite ready for the high mountains and suggested leaving my first participation in the Tour until 1976. While Merckx was winning his fifth tour, I was training rigorously with the prospect of the world championship in Montreal in mind. I was desperate to gain revenge for the fiasco that had taken place twelve months earlier in Barcelona.

As usual, on the night before the battle for the rainbow jersey, there was a meeting of all the Belgian riders. The traditional question was asked: "Who thinks they can win?" Almost as traditionally, nearly everybody put their hand up. Only my team mates and Merckx's domestiques abstained. The members of the federation, for their part, made clear that there was to be no racing behind any Belgian who had escaped.

I knew what I had to do then; make sure I was the first Belgian to get away, or otherwise I would have to help block attacks. When the Frenchman, Thevenet, went to the front, I went looking for him along with the Italian, Conti. That meant that three nationalities had to protect the break behind us. At least that was the theory, because as it turned out Merckx had paid the Dutchman, Roy Schuiten, to force a way through behind us. Despite his efforts we stayed out of reach. This time, though, he had arranged another way to stop me taking the world title. At a particular moment, the Flandria physio left the feeding station and someone made use of the opportunity to put something into my drinking bottle. The effect didn't take long to work, I got intestinal cramp and diarrhoea. At first I carried on riding but eventually I became so weak and dizzy that I had to get off and retire. There was no way it could have been exhaustion and to me it was clear that someone had *stabbed me in the back*.

My enemies would easily be able to reject the above as a cheap excuse if it weren't for the fact that what I had suspected was confirmed afterwards. The perpetrator himself made it known. His name was Gust Naessens; he was the physio for Eddy Merckx at the time and later became my personal soigneur. He can't confirm the story himself any more as he died a couple of years ago, but he did admit to me that he had put something into my bottle that day to enable Merckx to win the rainbow jersey for the third time without any problems. During the world championship in Prague in 1981 Gust Naessens, my wife Carine and her young friend Christa swore not to leave the cool-box for a second. If one of them had to go to the toilet one of the others stayed behind sitting on the box to make sure my food and drink weren't tampered with. That's because Gust knew better than anyone else, from his own experience, that one moment of not paying attention was enough to allow foul play by a rival.

I also became much more wary following the Montreal incident. When I had signed in during a stage race I always make sure to take my drinking bottle around with me and never leave it on my bike, unguarded. A healthy sense of mistrust for my fellow man was not out of place here.

10   The arrival of the Godfather

The start of the 1975 season produced a similar scenario to the previous season. In the Tour of Andalusia I was the master in five of the stages and as a reward I collected the overall victory. In the Tour of Belgium I took three stages and the victory and this time it wasn't taken away from me. That was the cue for a number of journalists to put words in my mouth about how I was going to beat Merckx convincingly in the Tour of Flanders the following Sunday. I realise that through articles such as that they wanted to bring a certain *ambience* into cycling. Cultivating a rivalry between two top figures is always interesting, whether it be Van Steenbergen and Van Looy, Van Looy and Merckx, Merckx and Maertens or any other pair. Usually it's the youngest one of the two who ends up the victim of the jousting.

In the Tour of Flanders I only finished eighth, but three days later I came away with my very first victory in a classic when I won Ghent-Wevelgem. The wind always plays a major part in this race because much of the route is along the coast. The breezes cause a natural selection to take place and it pays to stay alert during the whole of the race. In the 1975 event, Tonny Stroucken took what I think is one of the best photos ever taken of me. At a particular moment when I'm at the front and looking to my right, Merckx and De Vlaeminck are alongside each other deliberating on how they can clip my wings. They didn't succeed in their goal, though. Living up to his reputation as the locomotive, Marc Demeyer towed me through to the sprint where I easily got past Frans Verbeeck and Rik Van Linden. That success gave me cause for double satisfaction. Not only did I have a classic against my name, something I'd yearned for for a long time, but I was also rehabilitated following my ignominious defeat in the Tour of Flanders where Merckx had once again proved superior.

Four days after Ghent-Wevelgem, I came 6th in Paris-Roubaix. I've never really had much luck in the 'Hell of the North.' Every rider has to change a wheel at some time or other, but with me it always seemed to happen at a bad time. Whether I was on form or not had nothing to do with it.

In the Dauphiné Libéré I won all the first six stages and then we were faced with two difficult mountain stages. Up to that point

Guillaume Driessens couldn't say enough nice things about me. He loved being around me when there was plenty of success. During the previous winter there had been discussions between Paul Claeys and him in which it was agreed in principle that he would manage the Flandria team in 1976. However, when I lost nearly half an hour around Chartreuse on the stage from Romans to Grenoble, Driessens didn't want to know me. The same thing happened the next day on the stage to Briançon over the Cols Croix-de-Fer, Télégraphe and Galibier. In the final time trial I managed to win again, even though it looked as though I was going to be denied through a piece of carelessness by my team-mate, Roger Verschaeve. He had been caught immediately by the rider who had started right after him and as a twosome they turned it into a sort of mini Baracchi Trophy. I only managed to put in a time a few seconds quicker than this other rider but Lomme Driessens, who I hadn't seen anywhere after the two mountain stages, was hanging around my neck again.

There was a particular reason why I lost so much time during the mountain stages. While carrying a heavy suitcase in my hotel room I twisted awkwardly and injured my back. When I told the journalists about it, naturally they didn't believe me. They wrote that I would never be able to stay with the leaders over the cols. I found articles like that totally unnecessary. I never thought of myself as a mountain goat, but at the same time I was convinced that in the Tour de France I would easily reach Paris if I concentrated on the green jersey rather than the yellow.

In spite of the back injury I went on to the Midi Libre. When Driessens found out he drove as fast as he could to the airport at Zaventem to try and convince me at the last minute that it would be better if I stayed at home. Flandria, however, insisted that I should ride and I boarded the plane. It turned out that Lomme had been right and the pain was so unbearable I couldn't start the second stage.

That season the world championship was to be held at Yvoir in Belgium. Although I had done plenty of training I knew beforehand that I wouldn't be able to turn in one of my better performances. Roger De Vlaeminck rode the best world championship of his career at Yvoir even though he didn't put on the rainbow jersey that day. The blame for that lay firmly at the door of the other Belgians, myself included. We held him in a vice and gave the Dutchman Hennie Kuiper carte blanche. Although I didn't rate my own chances of winning, Pollentier and myself did not accept Merckx's invitation to all the Belgian squad to go to his house for a discussion. There was absolutely no point. Why should we have to listen to the same litany as the previous year again? Whenever Merckx, who was always given enough personal helpers by the BWB, spoke, it was always for his own benefit.

I won both the autumn classics, Paris-Brussels and Tours-Versailles.

"Thanks to me," gloated Driessens afterwards.

That claim was only partly correct. Although I was in regular contact with Lomme regularly during the races, it was Briek Schotte who sat in the team car.

However during the winter of 1975-76 Driessens was appointed number one directeur sportif and Briek had to settle for running the B-team. What did I see in Lomme that made me allow Paul Claeys to demote Schotte? Well, although Driessens may have got up to everything at some time in his life, one thing has to be said for him: he could motivate like no-one else. Even when you felt terrible because you were riding badly, he could almost make you believe you were the best rider in the race.

In order to create the team that he wanted to build around me at Flandria for the 1976 season he brought in a number of young riders, who he hoped to be able to mould into shape. The difference between Driessens and Schotte was simply that Driessens would state clearly, 'Everybody rides for Maertens or your salary will be held back.' It was understood that if I was having an off day I had to make it known, so that Pollentier or Demeyer could take over straightaway.

One of Lomme's important weapons was that he had the gift of the gab. He was never short of a word or two, so much so that in cycling circles many felt he lived in a fantasy world. For example, he proclaimed with much ballyhoo that it was *he* who had made Coppi, Van Looy, Merckx and Maertens into champions. If you were to believe Driessens, even Monseré became world champion at Leicester thanks to him and him alone, even though that was actually a million miles from the truth. As for the others, there is definitely an element of truth – he *helped* make Coppi, Van Looy, Merckx and me. On the other hand you have to remember that he always picked the best riders to work with. Put a racehorse and a carthorse together on a stud farm and let Driessens train the carthorse. I don't think even Lomme could help it to win the Grand Prix de Vincennes.

Briek Schotte felt as if he had been shunted out, and for Walter Godefroot the arrival of Driessens at Flandria was the signal to start looking for another team as he wanted nothing to do with him as directeur sportif. Pollentier, though, accepted it from the off, while Demeyer had his doubts at first as he had always been Schotte's favourite. In the end however he became reconciled to Driessens' arrival, although this didn't stop the two of them clashing frequently. If Driessens was afraid of anyone it was muscleman Demeyer.

'Hang on *lad,* hang on,' Lomme would say to try to calm him down whenever Marc let him know that one of his suggestions hadn't gone down too well.

Driessens came round to my house nearly every day that winter and he would poke his nose into everything, even the way Carine ought to prepare food for me. Many other women would have definitely let him know quickly who was the boss in the kitchen, but Carine would keep quiet and patiently put up with the fact that even in her domain, he held sway. Her justification for it was that it was for Freddy's well being. She was still young as well, and nowadays she wouldn't put up with anyone interfering the way he did.

A few days after I won the Grand Prix des Nations in Angers in 1976 I was booked to ride a kermesse in Oostrozebeke.
'Why don't you come with me?' I asked Carine. 'My mother will do some supper for us tonight.'

As is customary among riders' wives, she sat in the car the whole afternoon and watched the race from there. I won, and after changing I went over to the car and said 'I'm just going to the prize giving ceremony then I'll be straight back. Will you wait here for me?'

Normally presentations like these are a formality and take place in a café bar (you give in your number and collect an envelope) and it only takes a few minutes. This time however, Carine was forced to wait no less than two hours for me. She had no idea why I hadn't come back. So why did it take me so long?

Lomme informed me only after the prize-giving that a reception was going to be held for us at the Town Hall and added that there was no need to go and get Carine as it wouldn't last very long. Actually Lomme preferred Carine staying in the car since it meant that he alone would be the one by my side as the tributes were being handed out. When I eventually got back to her and she found out what had happened, she was furious and quite rightly so. I couldn't claim to be blameless, it was just that in those days you carried out everything Lomme asked of you without question.

On one occasion I didn't stand for it though. After the world championship in Venezuela in 1977 Lomme, by way of an exception, allowed Carine to come with me to the Tour of Catalonia.

'You sit here alone at home the whole season, Carine,' he said.

'The trip abroad will get you out of your daily routine.'

Lomme would soon regret his obliging gesture.

Beside him Carine and me, a couple who were friends of Lomme, baker Victor Van Eeckhoudt and his girlfriend, travelled with us in the plane to the starting place, Sitges. When we arrived in the hotel it transpired that Lomme had organised it so that Carine would be sharing a room with the other woman.

'I'll share with Victor,' suggested Lomme. 'You'll be with another Flandria rider.'

'I'm not having this,' I said to Carine, "we're not schoolkids any more!' We grabbed our cases and went down to the foyer.

'Could you telephone the airport and find out when the first plane to Belgium departs please?' I asked the receptionist. Lomme stood there looking totally perplexed.

'But wait a minute, listen *lad*,' he stuttered while puffing on his cigar in panic.

In the end he did an about-turn and allowed Carine and me to sleep together every night. It didn't seem to do me any harm as I won five stages and overall victory in the Tour of Catalonia that year.

Lomme didn't have much time for riders' wives in general *'They shouldn't let themselves get involved and should just make sure they can cook a nice minestrone soup for their husbands,'* he would declare to anyone who happened to be listening. If there had been a union of riders' wives, and they had held a referendum among the members to find out who in the cycling world was the most unfriendly to women, it would have been a foregone conclusion who would have won.

One evening I came home with Lomme and Marc Demeyer after a race. That morning Lomme had said that he wouldn't be staying but would be going back home to Vilvoorde straightaway. While we were out Carine and her friend Christa, who often used to stay with us, had prepared a lovely meal for four people and they had even decorated the table with candles. When we walked in Carine and Christa hid themselves on the stairs hoping Lomme would soon be on his way. Unfortunately Lomme saw the four plates and, not knowing that the fourth plate was not meant for him but for Christa, invited himself for a hearty meal. All this time Carine and Christa were still sitting on the stairs getting really fed up at having to follow our conversation from a distance. After a good two hours, Lomme finally decided it was time he went home and headed for his car. Marc and I opened the door to the stairs straightaway and came across Carine and Christa who were almost at the point of passing out from hunger.

Oh dear, Lomme and women. Take the rest day during the 1976 Tour de France at Divonne-les-Bains where I was in the yellow jersey. On the previous evening Carine, Paul Claeys and his wife and the wife of Walter Verlé (assistant directeur sportif at Flandria) had arrived at our hotel after an exhausting car journey through the day's heat.

'Where can I find Freddy and Lomme?' Paul Claeys asked politely.

He was told by Walter Verlé that he had heard Lomme say to me, 'We'll make sure we've gone out before the women arrive. Let's go and have something to eat well out of the way.'

Paul Claeys wasn't very happy with this answer, naturally. Together with Verlé, who arranged that the four of them could stay at our hotel, the group set off for a restaurant. Once back at the hotel they found out that the other riders were already in bed but that there had been no sign of Lomme and me.

The next morning I rang Carine's room from mine. Up to then I still hadn't seen her.

'Where were you last night then?' Carine asked inquisitively. I explained to her that Lomme had lured me away.

'Are you annoyed?' I asked.

'No, I'm not annoyed,' she whispered.

'Get dressed quickly,' I said. 'I'll see you down in the garden at half past eight, before I have to go training with the team at ten o'clock.'

When I got to the garden, Carine, Paul Claeys and his wife were already waiting there. A pack of press photographers was also present, eager to take the opportunity to get a few typical rest-day snapshots.

Then all of a sudden Lomme, cigar in mouth, rolled up roaring, 'Maertens, if you're planning to train with us today, get yourself off to the other riders now. Got that?'

There had been nothing to bring on this show of venom except, of course, for the fact that for once he wasn't the centre of attention.

'You go.' Carine suggested, just to avoid any more trouble.

'See you this afternoon!' I said. 'We won't be disturbed then and we can go for a nice walk. Just the two of us.' When we got back from training I waved to Carine from my bike.

'See you soon,' I called. 'I've just got to go and have something to eat with the other riders first.' She understood only too well what that might mean.

After lunch, Carine strolled down to the park with Paul Claeys and his wife. She asked some of the other riders who were hanging round there,

'Have any of you seen Freddy and Lomme anywhere?'

'Lomme went off with Freddy, Pollentier and Demeyer in his car,' one of them was able to inform her.

He was right as well. Lomme had said to us, 'Let's get away from all the hustle and bustle,' and with that he whisked us off to a restaurant across the border in Geneva. Afterwards, he made us go and relax in a wood where we lay with our legs resting upwards against a tree.

It wasn't until 5.30 that evening that we turned up back at the hotel. I explained to Carine that I hadn't been able to warn her in advance of what was likely to happen and once again she understood.

A little later, Lomme whispered to her as if he was hatching a plot, 'Don't say a word to anyone, but if you want you can go to Freddy's room and you can have an hour alone together.'

Carine was taken totally by surprise at such a show of generosity by Lomme, but she wasn't to know then the trick he was about to play. When Carine walked into my room I was delighted that at long last the two of us could just have a quiet chat. She had hardly been with me for five minutes, though, when Lomme suddenly appeared with Jacques Anquetil.

'Look who's come to say hello,' cracked Lomme. 'None other than Jacques Anquetil! Take a chair and sit down, Jacques. Freddy's got plenty of time to have a natter with you.'

Lomme left without giving a thought to Carine. Later, the door opened and he announced, 'Right *lad*, it's time for your evening meal.'

The next morning it was the stage to Alpe d'Huez. Before the start I just had time to give Carine a quick kiss before we parted and she had to accept that as her only reward for the long journey she had made. We had been alone together for precisely five minutes on that rest day.

Sex and sporting performance. Everyone knows the stories about what kind of a negative influence the former may have on the latter. Opinion is divided on the issue but I always believed in the theory in as much as I never 'partook' for three days before an important race.

That was the reason that on one night during the first year of our marriage, Carine was reduced to floods of tears. We went to bed and Carine was hoping that I would make a move but I was having none of it.

'Leave me alone will you?' was all I said and Carine couldn't understand why.

'What's wrong Freddy?' she asked. 'Are you mad at me?'

'No, you must just leave me to rest.'

'At least tell me what's the matter,' Carine insisted, as she can never understand it when people are off-hand without her knowing why.

'Stop nagging me!' I replied, making my way to the spare bedroom.

Carine came after me, crying. She must have imagined that I had already fallen for someone else.

'I'll explain everything to you some other time,' I said trying to calm her down. 'Now, just go to bed and try to get some sleep.'

At a later date I made sure I explained to her that although the will had been there that night, I couldn't allow myself to do anything with the Tour of Flanders just around the corner. Some professionals, Gimondi for example, were much stricter about it than I was judging from what they said, and they maintained their self-discipline over a long period, but I never took it that far. For instance, on the day of a classic I would definitely *do it* that evening. In stage races, the fact that my wife wasn't there didn't make me feel as though I was missing out on it. Everything was geared towards the race and I was so busy day and night that I simply never thought about it.

However, I'd be the last to claim that during these stage races we riders lived like monks from start to finish. During the 1975 Dauphiné Liberé, in which I won seven stages, Carine and Michel Pollentier's wife Josiane were guests one evening in the tour caravan. While we were having a meal, the hostesses from Radio Monte Carlo came up to Michel and me and lifted their T-shirts for us to sign their well-formed breasts.

"Are you two always so courteous?" asked our two other halves.

Their suspicions were not misplaced. While they stayed alone at home, their husbands were gallivanting around on their own abroad, with the knowledge that all around them – especially if they were top riders – were all sorts of women; beautiful and ugly (but mostly beautiful). The reader shouldn't let his imagination run away with him too much here. You were in the public eye so you really had to be on your guard against scandal. As soon as the journalists got a sniff of anything you could be sure it would spread like wildfire.

We are still men though, in the prime of life and in peak condition, so occasionally it could be expected that we would overstep the mark. In 1977, Marc Demeyer and I rode in the Milan Six Days. Roger De Vlaeminck and Ronald De Witte were also there, riding as a duo. Lomme wanted to collect Marc's money and mine and De Vlaeminck said to him, "Take our cash with you as well, we're all going back to the hotel straightaway."

However, the hotel proprietor drove us off to a dimly lit bar in the city and dropped us off there.

After we'd been there about an hour and a half, *Signore Maertens* was suddenly required on the telephone. It seemed Lomme had grabbed the hotel owner by the scruff of the neck and

Freddy displays the collection of trophies and jerseys he had accumulated by the age of 16.

More jerseys on display as Freddy and wife Carine pose before their first house in 1974.

One of the great disappointments in Maertens' career. His last-ditch effort to catch Felice Gimondi is thwarted, and victory in his world championship debut at Barcelona in 1973, eludes him. Eddy Merckx – showing more than a passing interest in Maertens' efforts – trails in 4th behind Luis Ocana. (*Hulton–Deutsch*)

The podium after the race. Resigned looks on the faces of Maertens and Ocana, flanking the winner Gimondi. (*Photosport International*)

A classy line up on the cobbles during Paris–Roubaix in 1975. Merckx, Godefroot, Guido Van Sweevelt, Maertens, André Dierickx – in the background – and Roger De Vlaeminck. (*Photosport International*)

Action from the Flèche Brabançonne in 1975 and, as ever, Maertens is keeping a close watch on Eddy Merckx.

In the Tour of Belgium in 1975, Maertens took three stages and overall victory. Here he is seen being led to the podium.

During the same event a bloodied and stunned Maertens being brought around by, among others, physio Jef Dhondt after a sprint finish crash.

The Flandria team were also in demand as footballers. Here they are seen lined up for a team photo before the start of a game against a café team in 1976. How many do you recognise?

Action from the match suggests Freddy made the right sporting decision when he chose a career in cycling.

In his Tour de France debut in 1976, the red jersey of Flandria was soon traded for the yellow jersey of the overall leader, but in the end it was green which Maertens was to wear into Paris.

After winning the Baracchi Trophy in 1976, the Flandria entourage enjoy a celebratory meal. From left to right: Maertens, Jef Dhont, Michel Pollentier, Jules Nijs, Mr Boon and Lomme Driessens.

Freddy and his wife Carine in Majorca at the Flandria training camp in 1976. (*Photosport International*)

threatened to kill him if he didn't immediately tell him where we were.

First of all De Vlaeminck went to the phone.

"I've got nothing to say to you!" screamed Lomme, foaming with rage. "I want to speak to *my* rider."

When I had finished on the telephone, my tail was firmly between my legs. Lomme had given me exactly half an hour to be back at the hotel, or else . . .

I've always been honest with Carine when it comes to anything like that. She was well aware that that sort of thing would never happen in the middle of a season – during the Tour de France for instance. At the very most it was once during a training camp or after the Tour of Lombardy when there were no more races to come, or after a criterium abroad. We'd just let ourselves go simply as a form of reaction. One thing leads to another at times like that when a few men get together over a beer. It doesn't take long before you start eyeing the women. 'If there were no bad women, there would be no bad men,' is how Carine sees it and I reckon she's right.

Top sportsmen in general shouldn't have to behave more like saints than they really are. Anyway, put a hundred businessmen (or a hundred journalists) in a line and ask them if any of them have never done anything improper. Just see what answers you get.

11   A United Effort

The 1976 season was the most successful in my cycling career. After Het Volk the Flandria team under Lomme Driessens moved on to Paris-Nice where I won six stages. I never had a better chance of winning Milan-San Remo than I did that year. On the descent of the Poggio, one of my tyres blew just as I had escaped with Merckx and De Vlaeminck. Two days later I was luckier and victory was mine in the Flèche Brabançonne. In the closing stages of the race Merckx came up to me to ask if I would let him win.

"I'm riding in front of my own people," was the case he put forward.

"I'm riding in front of my own people as well," I answered. "We're both Belgians!"

Then he tried to frighten me by saying there would be a dope control afterwards. Why should that have worried me though? I wasn't afraid of it even though I knew the person in charge of it, the son-in-law of Frans Ceulaers, chairman of the national sport committee of the BWB, was a good friend of Merckx.

I took the top prize in the Amstel Gold Race as well, in what was my first race after the Fleche Brabançonne. Unfortunately, the Tour of Flanders turned out to be an anti-climax. Five of us were at the front: Roger De Vlaeminck, Francesco Moser, Walter Planckaert, Marc Demeyer and me. Then De Vlaeminck managed to put me out of the race by using a psychological trick. He stopped taking his turn at the front and I was worried that he was up to something. At a certain moment, I left a gap behind Demeyer, Moser and Planckaert to force De Vlaeminck to close it, but he just stayed where he was. While we were watching out for each other Demeyer looked round wondering what was going on and gave me a clear signal with his arm that I shouldn't hesitate any longer. I was determined not to pull the irons out of the fire for De Vlaeminck though, and as it turned out, Planckaert had the last laugh. In the sprint, Moser and Demeyer didn't stand a chance against him.

After the race Demeyer was furious, and rightly so: I had been taken in completely. Instead of confidently taking Marc's wheel, I'd let myself be fooled like a small child. Marc wasn't the only one who was displeased, either. Paul Claeys summoned me indignantly to his office in Zedelgem. As usual, I had to wait an age in reception before he would see me. If anything was going wrong in the team, I was always the one held responsible. That day, he shrieked *'Country bumpkin!'* at me.

In an interview with the weekly magazine *Sport 70,* which came out on the Tuesday after the Tour of Flanders, Briek Schotte was quoted as saying that I had ridden like a *caveman* and that I had behaved like an *ass.* It must be said that this criticism needs to be seen in the light of his demotion to manager of the B team, but nevertheless I protested to him personally against the statement by registered letter. Just like me, Briek was an employee of Flandria and as such should not have made comments like that about a colleague in public. At the root of his spite was, of course, that it was *his own* Marc Demeyer whose pride had been hurt. Briek was of the opinion that, "If Marc hadn't sacrificed himself, he could have won the race."

It's easy to say something like that. Dutch cabaret artist, Freek de Jonge, wrote a good song about it, *The "If" Waltz,* in which he sings, *'If it hadn't have been for my father . . . or my mother . . . if it hadn't have been for my father with my mother . . . I would be unrecognisable and I would have been irrepressible.'* Everything was always if, if, if. If I'd been called Martens instead of Maertens, I would have been the Prime-Minister of Belgium for years now.

One final word on the subject though – Marc Demeyer was right. I made a mistake and that is simply one of the risks of being the team leader. Your responsibilities involve taking decisions which sometimes turn out to be the wrong ones. This pressure should never be underestimated. *It's lonely at the top.* When I became champion of Belgium in Dilsen in 1976 I was expected at the works factory the next day. In the showroom I bumped into Paul Claeys' brother-in-law who was a director of the concern's Zwevezele branch where mopeds and gas convectors were made.

"Hello Freddy," he said. "Haven't you been riding in many races recently? It's ages since I last saw your name at the top of the results page."

"That's right, Mr. Van Merris," was all I said even though I really felt like giving him an earful. I mean, for crying out loud, it was only the day before that I'd become national champion and sir was asking if I was still racing.

Three days after the Tour of Flanders I won in Ghent-Wevelgem. Before the start, the name 'Velda,' who had become our co-sponsor at the last moment, needed to be sewn quickly on to our jerseys. In this classic, which was ravaged by storms and snow, I tried to get to the front on my own so that I could attack on the Kemmelberg. However, I could only stay in front of the group of pursuers for 15 kilometres, and it was only in the sprint that I was able to finish the job off. After the race Lomme caused a sensation once again. He announced into the microphone of BRT radio journalist, Marc Stassijns, his retirement from cycling. The news exploded like a bomb. In actual fact Lomme didn't have the slightest intention of quitting and he only wanted to put Paul Claeys under pressure finally to remove Briek Schotte from the scene following his remarks about the final stages of the Tour of Flanders. Barely half an hour after Lomme had announced his resignation, he had changed his mind again.

"Lomme, it's terrible the way you are leaving us in the lurch," we added to keep the comical aspect going.

"All right then, since you asked me so nicely, I'll carry on," Lomme was quick to respond even though we hadn't pressed him at all.

He then immediately telephoned the BRT sports editor to correct the report, which they had already broadcast. What *hasn't* Lomme announced in his time? He always used to say that *he* had been world champion on a number of occasions when of course he actually meant *his riders*.

One of the funniest anecdotes involving him took place when the team was all together in the seclusion of the Hotel De Kroon in Ninove. Normally Paul Claeys would let the ten riders drink a couple of bottles of wine together in the evening, but on this occasion Lomme was in a stroppy mood and wouldn't allow it.

"I'm going to take a sauna," he announced all of a sudden "They're good for my health."

That was just the opportunity we had been waiting for. As soon as he was in the sauna, we barricaded the door and gleefully sat down at the table to drink a glass of wine. When we let Lomme out after an hour, he looked more like a boiled lobster than a directeur sportif.

"I feel much better for that," he claimed, as if nothing had happened; yet for some reason he never mentioned that he'd spent nearly the whole time banging on the door of the sauna.

On another occasion there was a Flandria team training session and we were supposed to change in the dressing rooms at the SC Lombardsijde football ground. On the way there Lomme called in at our house. I couldn't believe my eyes when I saw him arrive with his head the colour of a beetroot and all the skin flaking off it.

"What on earth's happened?" I asked.

"Terrible isn't it, *lad*," he answered in all seriousness. "I used the wrong tube of ointment."

Later I found out what had actually happened. Lomme always liked to have a nice tan (during a stage race abroad he would always have a massage) and on his own initiative he had used an infra-red lamp like physiotherapists use to warm up riders' muscles, only he had sat in front of it for far too long.

When Marc Demeyer triumphed in Paris-Roubaix in 1976, much of the credit should go to the tactical skill of Driessens. I had fallen and was actually lying in hospital but Lomme made out that I was following behind so that the group of four escapers, Moser, De Vlaeminck and Kuiper would think it only natural that Marc would not do any lead work. In the sprint he was still fresh enough to beat them all.

It has been said that this marked the beginning of a cooler relationship between Marc and me, but this isn't true. How could I begrudge him his win after I had been put out of the race by a crash? Once again it was journalists who started this rumour because they saw it as a way to come up with a few interesting articles. Perhaps some of them felt that things were going too well in the Flandria team. After the Tour of Flanders, the headlines in *Sport 70* were '*Marc Demeyer is too big a champion to remain a domestique.*' It wasn't this, however, that was to turn Marc's head. That was not to happen until after the 1978 season.

The two Walloon classics almost provided me with a double celebration. In the Flèche Wallonne, I ended 3rd but in Liège-Bastogne-Liège I would never have lost in normal circumstances. Joseph Bruyère and Herman Van Springel (who by now was riding for Flandria) were together at the front. Van Springel called Driessens to him, though, and told him that he didn't want

65

to win as he wanted to avoid the dope control. Lomme came back to us, the chasing group, where we had been checking any attacks the whole time, to let us know what was going on straightaway. It was only then that we went after Bruyère, while Van Springel had let us overtake him in the meantime. At the finishing line, we had failed by half a minute to catch the Walloon and I won the sprint for 2nd place.

On 1st and 2nd May I did celebrate a double successs with victories in the Henninger Turm in Frankfurt and in the Championship of Zurich. These were to be beyond my expectations as I had gone along with the plan to let Roger De Vlaeminck win in Zurich as he really needed a classic win. On one of the climbs, however, De Vlaeminck suddenly let Walter Godefroot pull away. Ronald De Witte, who at that time was a team-mate of De Vlaeminck, couldn't understand why and in his annoyance he reacted. I was even more angry because De Vlaeminck had obviously tried to *stab me in the back* for the benefit of Godefroot who was the last person Driessens wanted to see win. In the final kilometres De Witte asked me if the agreement was still in force. I answered in the negative and paid the Italian, Marcello Bergamo, to lead out the sprint for me which I won. During the dope control De Vlaeminck was so irate that he almost flew at me. As far as I'm concerned it was his own fault he had lost: he had tried to *stab me in the back*. Suppose De Vlaeminck and Godefroot's ploy had come off, they would have been quite happy to have watched me suffer, wouldn't they?

That year I won the final overall classification in the Dunkirk Four Days. This short stage race which I was to win four times in all will always hold special memories for me. It was during this event that I beat Merckx in a time trial for the first time. In actual fact I could have won it five times if Walter Godefroot hadn't thrown a spanner in the works for me in 1974. In one of the stages the Frenchman, Fussien, had attacked right from the start. As the leader in the general classification I was obliged to shoot after him, taking another rider with me. It only appears to have got back to Merckx that I was involved in the breakaway after we had a lead of around forty seconds. In an instant, the Molteni team made its move and Godefroot, who was still the captain of Flandria, gave instructions to our team not to counter any attacks. The three of us still managed to keep the now unleashed pack twenty five seconds behind us though. However, when I had a puncture, the service car wasn't close enough to me and I had to just hope that things would turn out all right. The two others were also swallowed up, and when Godefroot saw his chance there was hardly any reaction and he built a lead of several minutes without any trouble. Merckx had got what he wanted, therefore; Maertens had lost. Spurred on by this I took my revenge in the time trial that afternoon but over a distance of little over 12 kilometres I obviously couldn't make up the deficit from that morning.

In the 1976 Tour of Switzerland everything went well – even in the mountains. This tour is usually greatly underestimated compared with the Tour de France, the Giro and the Vuelta. It's a mistake to do that, though, since the organisational strategy means the Tour of Switzerland is a tricky event. So much money is available in the primes – they are literally *golden sprints* – and there are so many different classifications being battled for at the same time that the tempo never slips. The Giro, on the other hand, is completely different. Italian teams control the proceedings at the start and keep a moderate pace going until the final stages when the pace increases dramatically.

After the Tour of Switzerland I arrived back in Belgium in peak condition and I took the national jersey at Dilsen. At the start Jos Jacobs and Marc Demeyer went to the front but Driessens instructed Marc not to do any lead work. At the same time the team manager of IJsboerke, Willy Jossaert, instructed Godefroot to sit on my wheel. On a cobbled section I managed to shake off my shadow and attacked. I was amazed to see who the rider was who stayed with me: Eric De Vlaeminck, Roger's brother. He had been going through all kinds of personal problems and it seemed as though he wanted to wipe them all out in one go with a top performance. Eventually, though, he had to let go as well. While Pollentier and Van Springel were nipping any counter-attacks in the bud in an exemplary way, I was gradually pulling away and after a solo effort of more than 30 kilometres I reached the line with a victory margin of 39 seconds ahead of Jean-Luc Vandenbroucke.

It cannot be denied that the first season with Driessens in charge has to be regarded as an unqualified success. Apart from the sporting side of things one of Lomme's achievements was that he made me less of a blabberer and into someone who considered his words before opening his mouth. Bearing in mind that Lomme did all my talking for me anyway, anything else would have been unlikely. What could I have possibly added? He decided who we could and couldn't talk to. If you weren't one of Lomme's *comrades* you didn't get anywhere near Pollentier, Demeyer or me. If necessary he would stand guard outside our door to make sure they didn't. Once, we crushed some sleeping pills into a powder and put it into the grated cheese he had with his soup so that, just for once, we could escape from his protection.

"It's a long time since I've felt as tired as I do today," yawned Lomme.

"Well, you're not a youngster anymore," we answered. "A nap will probably bring you round again."

Lomme went to his room and we listened to see if he was asleep. We then removed the key from the inside and locked him in so that he couldn't come looking for us as soon as he awoke.

During our stay in Venezuela for the world championships in 1977 the three of us had hired a car so that we could go out after the title race without him knowing. Lomme thought it expedient on that warm summer's evening to take up position on a chair outside our room, a large cigar hanging from his mouth. Our room was in the basement and while Pollentier, who had broken his collarbone on a training ride on the circuit, was as silent as the grave, Demeyer and I clambered outside through the grating. As we drove past in the car, we sounded the horn to Lomme who gave the people inside a friendly wave without having a clue who they were.

The next morning he told us, "Do you lot want to hear something? Last night while you were all asleep I was sitting here outside your room when suddenly a car went past full of people waving at me. It's amazing to think that my face is so well known that people even recognise me on the other side of the world, isn't it?"

As already mentioned, a journalist had to be a *friend* of Lomme if he wanted to speak to us. The annoying thing was that Lomme changed *friends* all the time so that in the end you never knew who you were and were not allowed to speak to. One day somebody would be his *friend* but on the next you weren't even allowed to say hello to him. After the Grand Prix des Nations in 1976 for example, I was ordered to say nothing to Théo Mathy from RTBF television because on that particular day he was not one of Lomme's friends. Being protected from journalists in this way did me more harm than good. Whenever one of these newspaper writers, who would claim they were simply 'doing their jobs,' had the chance to write a venomous piece about me, they never let the opportunity pass.

At one point Lomme insisted that Carine and I should go and live in Brussels. Although I was in complete agreement with his reasoning that living in a more central place would reduce travelling greatly, I was also afraid that he would be round at our house more often, giving Carine advice on the best way to prepare minestrone soup. In the end we decided to stay in Lombardsijde.

According to Lomme, as team leader I had to act in a more authoritative way to the others in the team, but that was not my style. I never talked about *servants* since to me it sounded like something from a byegone era. No, to me they were helpers and team-*mates*. During a race I would give instructions of course, but before and after a race any of them could say what they felt. They weren't treated any differently by Lomme than Pollentier, Demeyer and me, apart from the fact that they didn't have to cope with any responsibility. In longer stage races I tried to win as many stages as possible because that brought rewards for the whole team.

It was only in exceptional circumstances that I didn't go all out – like in the 1976 Tour de France when at Lomme's request I gave the Frenchman, Jacques Esclassan, a rider with the French Peugeot team which had hardly done anything up to then, the present of a stage win. Once over the line, the journalist Louis Clicteur came after me holding his nose, as if hinting at the singeing smell coming from my brake blocks. He wasn't the only one who had noticed there was a funny smell in the sprint. I regretted it afterwards because if I had won it would have brought my total number of stage wins in the 1976 Tour to 9 and I would have held the record on my own.

Perhaps I wasn't the only Flandria team member with something to complain about at the time. We changed our tactics after that and one of the stages in the 1977 Paris-Nice provides a perfect illustration of the new plan. As Flandria were generally regarded as the strongest team, our rivals always expected us to do all the work in the chasing group. As soon as we had countered an attack another one would quickly follow so, as it was very energy sapping for us, we decided to do things differently. In this particular stage during Paris-Nice, three riders were out in front. Instead of immediately closing the gap, we pretended that we were unable to catch them, while at the same time making sure we never fell more than thirty seconds behind. It's true, it wasn't unusual for me to restrain my team-mates and in this way let the other riders have a wheel to see in front of them. It was then only in the last ten kilometres that with one big push we would shoot up to the leaders. Pollentier and Demeyer then kept up such a fierce pace that nobody could escape and I would round off the action. I don't think the way the three of us were so often in a position to manipulate the closing stages so much to our own advantage has been matched in cycling since then.

12   Green with a dark shadow

Four days after the 1976 national championships at Dilsen I
started in my first Tour de France. I rode the prologue in Merlin
Plage with a gear of 55x12, something I'd never done up to then.
It turned out to be the first of eight stage victories in that Tour.
I've already mentioned that I sold a stage to Jacques Esclassan
and if I hadn't been boxed in on the Champs Elysées, where
Dutchman Gerben Karstens was the quickest, I would have won
there as well. Karstens always pulled a dirty trick from up his
sleeve, though. When you were bearing down on the finishing line
in his company, you were never sure what he would get up to
next.

I began the Tour with the aim of pinching as many stages as I
could, to keep the green jersey to Paris and to ride into Belgium
wearing yellow. Even the last one of the three came off that year.
I wore the *maillot jaune* until Divonne-les-Bains and this brought
with it the unavoidable and difficult task of controlling the action
in the whole race, while at the same time having to go in for all the
bonus sprints that counted toward the green jersey. To this day I
still maintain that if Driessens had informed me accurately about
what was going on during the stage from Divonne-les-Bains to
Alpe d'Huez, I wouldn't have lost the yellow jersey there. Joop
Zoetemelk took the stage and Lucien Van Impe took over the
overall lead. That night I was only 54 seconds behind him on the
general classification. The previous winter Michel Pollentier and
I had been on holiday in the region around Alpe d'Huez and had
familiarised ourselves with the notorious col.

When the tour caravan reached Montgenèvre the Alps were
out of the way and the Pyrenees loomed ahead. Before the stage
to Saint-Lary-Soulan, at the top of the Pla d'Adet, I was worried.
Van Impe, who won the stage by a margin of over three minutes
on Zoetemelk, should light a candle there for me. While Ocana,
who had come to an arrangement with Van Impe, gave him a tow
from the front, a keen battle was taking place in the background
between the team manangers of Van Impe (Guimard), of
Zoetemelk (Caput) and Driessens. They were all riding alongside
each other negotiating deals. If I had offered support to
Zoetemelk on that long winding road to Saint-Lary-Soulan, it

would have made a big difference as the Dutchman was clearly still fresh. However, I didn't ride at the front in spite of Caput's pleas and Zoetemelk's promise to reward me financially for my efforts. I wasn't interested because I feared a backlash from the Belgian public. The Barcelona affair had made me enough enemies, so the last thing I wanted now was to take any blame if my efforts were going to stop Van Impe winning the Tour.

That day I had two punctures during the closing stages and into the bargain I was also sent the wrong way. Without all that I would have finished 5th instead of 7th. After the Pyrenees I won another four flat stages and finished 8th in the final classification. Before the start in Merlin Plage I would never have said out loud that I would end up in so high a position.

Daily life in the Tour. Good co-ordination with the team personnel is essential so that whenever you arrived in an hotel you only needed to be massaged, to be given a solid meal and for the rest of the time to be left in peace. Credit must be given where it's due: thanks to Driessens the machine always ran like clockwork. He made sure that we could go to bed without worrying about practical things. The only thing we needed to do was to go through the stage schedule thoroughly and consult with team-mates about which gears we were going to be using. Riding with the same cogs was important for those occasions when we needed to change wheels. We didn't have anything else to worry about and when we rose in the morning everything had been sorted out for us. The Driessens organisation, among whom were physio Jef Dhont, his assistant Luc Landuyt and mechanic Freddy Heydens, made sure of that. Hats off for the way they coped with things, as it wasn't always a picnic for them.

During transfers I always slept well and this was a great advantage to me compared with many other riders. I even slept well in the car. After the Henninger Turm in 1976, which I had won, Lomme and I attended a reception in the Henninger brewery and as a result missed the plane which was supposed to take us to Zurich. Lomme drove the car there himself with me as passenger. We arrived at our hotel at three in the morning and only a few hours later I was due to start again (and I won again). Michel Pollentier who I always shared a room with was also a deep sleeper in spite of my snoring.

"You've sawn down a small wood again, you know!" was how he would greet me in the morning.

We never had time to become bored during the many kilometres that we rode day after day, as our team had to stay on the alert the whole time. Each rider was aware of his role in the team and knew there was a great deal to be earned. My yellow and green jerseys brought us money every day and we battled for the yellow and green caps (which were awarded for the team classification), there was also the scramble for points (for primes) and we received an extra bonus from Flandria for stage wins. If our domestiques had been keeping their eyes open during the stage, they would find that they had been riding for a great deal of money at the end of it. Riders like Pol Verschuere, Herman Beyssens and the Swiss Eric Loder probably look back on those days with great pride.

There was little chance to enjoy the marvellous landscape. People sometimes say to me, "You've seen a great deal during your career, haven't you!"

I answer back. "Actually I've *missed* more!" Not least when I was coming up to a mountain which I still had to climb.

"Encore un kilomètre!" the French would shout along the climb. Then you would get round the bend and to your great disappointment you would see that the top was still not in sight. In fact, what was even more dispiriting was the sign at the foot of the col saying *'Grand Prix de la montagne'* and next to it it would say how many kilometres there were to the top. The French cycling fans were certainly jovial and were not as over-the-top in their chauvinism as the myth would have you believe. The non-climbers who formed the 'bus' together at the back could count on as much sympathy from the public as the leaders.

Stages which took in three cols with a finish at the top of the third were particularly murderous. Some people call it a *mug's game* and maybe it is a bit. You had to know yourself and make sure you didn't waste energy unnecessarily. I never accepted the drinks that were offered to me as, for two reasons, this could prove dangerous. Firstly there was the chance that it would make you sick, and secondly, it may have contained a banned substance which would make you give a positive sample at the dope control without being aware of it. You also had to make sure you weren't pushed. A course commissioner in the car watched you closely, always ready to penalise you if he felt it necessary. It was a question, then, of making a clear gesture with your arm behind your back that you didn't want pushing, while at the same time shouting *"poussez! poussez!"* without being noticed.

In the morning our breakfast began with one of Lomme's recipes. He even got up first to prepare it – cream cheese mixed with honey and two egg-yolks. It didn't look very appetising but it tasted lovely! Lomme only took a small suitcase with him when he went abroad (the personnel washed their underwear and socks in an evening) and was always grumbling about how much luggage we were dragging around with us. One evening we cut the legs off a pair of his trousers that had been hanging on a chair. The next morning we didn't need to be woken up as we were all ready to watch his reaction to the discovery from behind the door.

"Who's done this?" moaned Lomme. "I don't think that's very nice, is it?" Upon which he instructed Jef Dhondt to go into town in the team car to get him a new pair of trousers.

After each stage victory, with Paul Claeys' permission, there was champagne on the table for us and during the meal we were allowed to have a glass of wine. This wasn't one of Driessens' initiatives as we had been doing the same thing during the Tour of Andalusia when Briek Schotte was still the manager. To an outsider it may have looked as though Flandria used to party into the small hours in these tours, but that would have been impossible. If we had have carried on like that we would never have lasted three weeks. While we are on the subject, later on it was often said how much I liked a drink but, for example, I used to deliberately refuse to take part in the traditional 'End of Season Race' at Putte-Kapellen. It is generally accepted that this where riders get a chance to go on a spree and after a gruelling season it's hardly surprising. Some riders even collect a starting number but don't actually start. Instead, they shout from the door of the bar they are in to lads who do feel like riding. That's one place where you would never see me, though.

Talking of champagne: whatever the race, if I was feeling good in the closing stages, I would always have half a drinking bottle of champagne with a quantity of fructose and an ampoule of caffeine mixed in thirty kilometres before the finish. It had a stimulating effect on my body although this was clearly not the case for everybody. Pollentier tried it out in the Baracchi Trophy in 1976 but got the *hunger knock*. During each stage of the Tour, one of my team-mates would drop back to the team car where the champagne was kept in a cool box and would bring the drinking bottle to me. The rider who liked doing this most was Herman Beyssens as he always used to have a sip out of it on the way back. Incidentally, Lomme would finish the bottle off from behind the steering wheel.

After I had my champagne I really would *fly*, as witnessed on the penultimate stage of the 1976 Tour on the stage to Versailles. As the weather was lovely when we started I rode on extra light tyres weighing only 190 grams. However, as soon as we reached the Chartreuse Valley it began to rain. I had escaped with Ferdinand Bracke and it looked as though nobody fancied getting a reaction going behind us. This meant that I could even start to think about setting my sights on 4th place in the final classification. Bracke was also riding out of his skin as I had promised him the stage victory. All of a sudden I fell and noticed that my chain was in a real mess and I clearly had no option but to wait for the team car. While I was standing on the roadside, the peloton went past and I shouted to my team-mates "Two of you stay with me! The rest of you carry on at full power!"

The three of us succeeded in getting back to the peloton eight kilometres from the end and despite the great exertions I had made, I beat everyone in the sprint.

That Saturday evening Carine, my father, Paul Claeys and his wife were at the Sofitel where our team were staying. I was very happy that the Tour was nearly over, although there was still a time trial and a short stage finishing on the Champs Elysées to come the following day. The green jersey was safely mine already though. It amazed me just how calm Carine remained, it seemed as though my triumph had left her rather indifferent and that her thoughts lay elsewhere.

"Is there something the matter?" I enquired.

"No Freddy. Why do you ask?"

"Because you don't seem to be very enthusiastic to me," I answered.

"Oh, it's just that I'm a bit overcome by all the goings on and the honour you'll be receiving tomorrow," she smiled.

I was reassured by that and I didn't dwell on it any longer. Afterwards it became clear, however, why Carine had been acting strangely: A few days earlier, Giovanni, the seven year old son of Jean-Pierre Monseré, had been knocked down by a car while out on his bike and had died of his injuries in hospital the following night. Carine knew about it and so did my team-mates, the team personnel and the journalists (who had found out about it when telephoning their copy through to Belgium). In other words, the entire tour caravan knew but everybody had jealously kept the secret from me. I still feel grateful for that, to this day, because I wonder what would have happened to my concentration on the final two stages if things had been different, especially since Giovanni's accident had happened on a racing cycle that he had received from me.

On the Sunday afternoon, after the *cérémonie protocolaire* on the Champs Elysées, Lomme Driessens had given himself the unenviable task of informing me of the tragic news. Up to that moment I was in a euphoric state with eight stage victories (including that morning's time trial) behind me and as the winner of the points classification and holder of the green jersey for over a week. Then Lomme came up to me and in a hesitant voice began, "I've got some bad news."

The first thing that rushed through my mind was, "I've been found positive at the dope control"

"No, it's nothing to do with the Tour," Lomme went on carefully.

"Well, what is it then?" I asked fearfully. "Has something happened to my mother?"

"No," Lomme answered and informed me what had happened to Giovanni.

The news hit me like a hammer blow. The whole world, which had seemed such a wonderful place moments before, fell apart around me in seconds. I've never appreciated how relative fame and success are as in that Paris hotel on July 18th 1976.

That same evening I was taken home by my father, Carine, Raoul Bouve (a politician from Middelkerke, but above all a good friend) and his wife, but I was still reeling from the shock. We stopped at Arras to have something to eat but the atmosphere was still sullen and I couldn't stop asking questions to try and find out details about Giovanni's accident.

"The hardest part will be when you arrive back home in Lombardsijde," said my father and he was right.

76

In my home village, hundreds of people had poured into the market square waiting for the fanfare to welcome me back.

My first reaction was, 'No, I can't go through with it. I want to go home straightaway to be alone,' but my father and Raoul tried to convince me that I ought not disappoint my supporters.

When we arrived in Lombardsijde the fanfare started playing cheerful tunes and I had to get into an open-topped car which took me home past the enthusiastic, applauding fans. From the balcony, I managed to give the crowd a friendly wave before retiring, but I'm sure they understood.

The next day, I paid my last respects to Giovanni's body in the hospital in Bruges. The experience left me shattered but afterwards Carine and I visited his mother in Rumbeke. Annie was lying in a daze on a settee in the living room. As for me, I was so distressed that I couldn't bring myself to go and see her at first, so Carine tried to comfort her while I stayed in the kitchen.

That evening, at the criterium in Aalst, I was once again expected to be the big hero.

13   Una giornata particolare

Criteriums were the principal way of cashing in on winning the green jersey. Those few weeks after a Tour de France are often greatly underestimated by the public. Even when the peloton is flying round the circuit at fifty kilometres an hour, you can still hear the cry, 'Lazy swines!' All I can say is just try staying out in front with a great storming pack chasing after you! Another often heard cliché is that it is arranged beforehand who is going to win a criterium. Sometimes there is talk, I won't deny that, but if sombody tells someone else that he thinks he can win, he has to go out and prove it. With all the corners and bends, after which you always have to get going again, it is certainly not just a leisurely exhibition ride.

In spite of how much some riders hate the criteriums as a preparation for the world championship I've never thought of them as being a disadvantage. I always have a message afterwards (on long journeys, my physio would always come with me), I never stayed behind too long discussing the race afterwards, I made sure I always got enough sleep and, most important of all, I always trained about 150 kilometres a day with the world championship in mind.

At the start of my career, Jean Van Buggenhout held absolute control whem it come to criterium contracts. He certainly lived up to his reputation of being a 'Merckxist.' I can remember my first meeting with Van Buggenhout in a cafeteria on the quayside at Ostend in 1973. He presented me with over twenty contracts. I thought I was worth BF 10,000 per criterium in view of the fact that I had finished 2nd in the Tour of Flanders and had turned out to be the revelation of the season among the young riders. However, Van Buggenhout saw it differently.

"You either ride all the criteriums for BF 6,000 each or you don't ride in any of them," he said. "It's one or the other."

His totally despotic position was a fact, so without any consultation with race organisers he would allow all of Merckx's team-mates to start on the same money as me. I had a better relationship with Firmin Verhelst who took over from Van Buggenhout after the 1976 Tour de France. This was partly thanks to Lomme, who was familiar with Verhelst's business style and could therefore negotiate deals with him. The contracts were usually made out on the rest days of the Tour and the French managers, Piel and Doucet, would also be present at the negotiating table.

I once missed the start of the Acht van Chaam thanks to Verhelst and as a result lost 100,000 francs. He had put the wrong starting time on the contract and I was so furious I drove home like a madman along the motorway at over 200 kilometres an hour.

"Can't you go any faster?" asked my father who was a passenger in the car.

I completed my preparations for the world championships in Ostuni a week before with the Tour of the Netherlands. Before I set off for Italy I said to Carine, "The man who can beat me on Sunday will be the world champion."

She didn't travel with me (the only time she did was to Prague in 1981) but followed the proceedings on television at home in Lombardsijde with her sister Christine and her husband Lionel, her brother Rik, my brother Marc and Annie Monseré. My mother, who had been in troubled health as a kidney dialysis patient for quite a time, didn't come with me either. It seemed as though I was regarded as the man to beat from the results of the traditional 'predicting the winner' competition which took place among the 300 journalists assembled at Ostuni. I received 35% of the votes cast while Merckx received 20% and Moser 16%. The Belgian team that year consisted of Merckx, Bruyère, Godefroot, Verbeeck, De Muynck, Planckaert, Van Impe, Pollentier, Demeyer and me. There was no Roger De Vlaeminck as the BWB did not select him because he had disobeyed their instructions and did not take part in the world cyclo-cross championships the previous winter despite being selected.

Originally there was not going to be a meeting of the Belgian team on the Saturday evening, but at the last minute one was arranged. If a Belgian rider became the world champion, it was agreed that he was to pay BF 100,000 to his nine team-mates. That was the definite arrangement and everyone promised to ride for either Merckx or me, depending on how the race was developing. Even Godefroot, who after the national championship at Dilsen had once again been in fierce competition with me in the Tour of the Netherlands, was reconciled to the idea without any objections. I thought it was rather suspicious that the arrangement had been reached so easily, so I was doubly on my guard the following day. There was less unanimity when it came to Paul Claeys' demand that Driessens should drive the team car. It was only after much ballyhoo that the other team managers who were gathered there agreed to let him take charge of the Fiat.

In the first half of the race my two loyal lieutenants, Michel Pollentier and Marc Demeyer stayed by my side. They protected me from the wind and kept me at the front of the outstretched peloton. Merckx, though, still tried to put one over on me by attacking at the feeding station. Fortunately, I spotted it in time and from then on I never let him out of my sight.

Eventually there was a two man escape comprising Zoetemelk and Moser and they continued to pull further and further ahead.

"What shall we do?" Merckx and Godefroot asked me.

"We'll try and pull them back of course," I answered

To achieve this Merckx gave his number one helper, Bruyère, the job of setting a scorching pace at the front. I had more confidence in Van Impe, though, and when we could see the two leaders begin a 1½ kilometre climb 300 metres ahead of us, I said to him, "If you'll give me everything you can for a kilometre, keeping me out of the wind and on your wheel, I'll give you something on top of the 100,000 francs" (the amount has been omitted).

Lucien did what I asked of him and in sight of the top I shot away from his wheel. Only the Italian, Conti, grimly managed to hang on and was also able to catch his countryman, Moser, and the Dutchman, Zoetemelk, with me. It wasn't for long however, as when Moser shot down the descent, risking everything, both Conti and Zoetemelk had to let go.

Moser and I bore down on the finishing line together. He attacked twice, on both occasions after he had taken shelter behind a Citroen with the television camera. When he did it a third time, I had had enough.

"I'm not doing any more lead work," I made clear to him.

"I can see the chasers catching up on us," he said, trying to make me change my mind.

"Let them come," I answered. "I'm not afraid of them."

Then he changed his tack and offered me about 10 million

francs in Belgian money if I would let him win in front of his own people. I refused.

The only option left open to him was to start the sprint from a long way out. I didn't let this put me off my line, and using a 52x12 gear I jumped past him easily. I was the world champion. Fourth time lucky. Immediately after the race Merckx came to congratulate me. Even he had to concede that on the strength of my performances during that season I was a worthy rainbow jersey holder.

That evening the whole Belgian team celebrated my world title and Paul Claeys treated us to champagne. After the dope control, I returned to my room to find Marc Demeyer sitting there, already a little tipsy. Later on in the evening it was he who made sure that the *feeding* took place by fetching four more bottles from the bar every time he went. On the way Marc had to go through a swing door and he kept having a bit of trouble with it, so it came as no surprise to anyone when two bottles slipped out of his hands and smashed on to the floor.

Paul Claeys had to pay more than 100,000 francs at the end of the evening for all the champagne we had drunk. A week later, as a joke, he sent the bill to Marc's house and attached a note which laconically stated that the amount in question would be deducted from his following month's wages. That day, Marc drove to Zedelgem in record time.

It was Driessens' intention to make me a double world champion that year in Italy by entering me for the pursuit title. However I wanted nothing to do with it as I felt that the season had been strenuous enough already.

The day after Ostuni I started in a 150 kilometre race in Châteaulin for which I had signed a conract beforehand, with a proviso that the starting money would be greatly increased if I had won the world championship. That night at Zaventem airport there was the happy reunion with Carine. My father was waiting for me at home in Lombardsijde where a celebration party had been prepared. In the end though, Marc Demeyer and I slept at Driessens' house in Vilvoorde. Lomme for his part had laid on plenty of champagne for Jules Nijs, Victor Van Eeckhoudt and many other friends but my father was, understandably, extremely annoyed.

The next day I was the main attraction in the Acht van Brasschaat which was won by Merckx. The event organiser was pleased with that, and I didn't begrudge the man from Brussels his win. After the criterium I finally returned to Lombardsijde and, fortunately, my father soon got over his anger at me not returning home the previous evening. He put that down to Driessens and not his son.

An even more spectacular tribute to the one on that Tuesday evening was to take place in our village on Sunday, 31st October. To great public interest, various clubs and societies had evoked a picture of my life in a procession which was rounded off with a carriage in which sat my father, Carine and me.

My contract was not revised until the following season, but after Ostuni, Pollentier, Demeyer and I did immediately receive a win bonus from Flandria which we shared between the three of us. I have to be honest and say that when it came to our salaries, we had nothing to complain about at Flandria in those days. The problems in that direction only started when the fortunes of the firm took a downward turn.

I rounded off the 1976 season with a double by winning the Grand Prix des Nations in Angers on 3rd October and by finishing more than two minutes ahead of the specialist time trial partnership of Moser-Schuiten with Michel Pollentier in the Baracchi Trophy. My Super Prestige award was no longer in danger after my world title victory and at the same time I achieved the greatest number of victories ever gained by a professional in one season. There is still some doubt remaining about the exact number: some say *fifty-four,* while others say *fifty-five,* depending on whether victory in a time trial which had been added to the warm-up programme of a criterium is counted separately or not. Even if the more conservative view is taken and it is counted as fifty-four, it is still higher than the record set by Merckx in 1971. Some sources actually credit him with fifty-four wins that season, but that is clearly inaccurate. On closer study of that total, it can be seen that three track races (Voghern on 8th September, Villafranca on 9th September and Cordenone on 17th October) have been included, when offically they should not be. In actual fact Merckx only won *fifty-one* times in 1971. I have pointed this out here simply to take the opportunity of putting the record straight.

After Ostuni Driessens took out an option for me to improve on the world hour speed record set by Merckx at 49.431 kilometres in October 1972. I was already fully into the preparations for this event (the medical supervision was to be undertaken by Italian doctors) when Paul Claeys unexpectedly put a stop to it. He saw that the cycle displayed in the velodrome at Milan on which I was to attempt the record had been made by the Ernesto Colnago Company without *his* knowledge. His reaction, therefore, was easy to imagine: he wouldn't let me carry out the attempt.

Looking back on it perhaps I should be grateful to him. Who is to say? In actual fact I wasn't too disappointed when the project was shelved indefinitely. After the Grand Prix des Nations in Angers I realised only too well how exhausting the attempt would have been and the last thing I wanted was to suffer the next season as a result.

Then again, perhaps I should have stuck to my guns anyway, because I had such a good chance of success at the time. On a winding circuit at Le Touquet Plage, I had once completed a 37 kilometre time trial at an average speed of about 48 kph. The thing I feared most about a record attempt like this one was the monotony of spending an hour just riding laps of a velodrome in Mexico City. It was to take place there because, just like with Merckx, the attempt was to be made where climatic conditions were most favourable. We had already decided that we would build a fence around the track to shield it from the wind and sponsors had even been showing an interest in the event.

When Francesco Moser beat the world hour record in January 1984, I watched it full of great admiration. In terms of material he was better equipped than Merckx was in his day with disc wheels, a much lighter bike, aerodynamic clothing and so on and the medical supervision had been refined more, but that's beside the point. You can't blame anyone for evolving with technology and science. Anyone who talks about a *false picture* is being unreasonable. Just as unreasonable as anyone who tries to work out who was the greater rider of all time: Coppi or Merckx. He who *compares* is always wrong.

The only one thing which is certain is that Merckx's hour and Moser's hour were exactly as long as each other's.

14 My friend Roger

During the winter of 1976-77 I went hunting regularly as I always did during the close season. On one particular hunt, which had been organised by a friend of Jef De Saedeleer from the newspaper, *Het Nieuwsblad,* I discovered completely unexpectedly that Roger De Vlaeminck was there as well. On that day it didn't spoil my enjoyment but a few months later on a couple of occasions it certainly did. I really liked hunting as it took place in the healthy fresh air and because I also regarded it as a form of training. While I was walking about I always wore a hunting outfit which had been made heavier with weights. It was, therefore, not only a form of relaxation, but also a way of maintaining my physical condition at the same time.

Before the opening of the cycling season proper in 1977 I took part in several track meetings. My victory in the national derny championship was my first official Belgian track title. I won the Six-Days at Antwerp with Patrick Sercu, and riding with Marc Demeyer I was 2nd in the Milan Six Days where we had sold the victory to Gimondi and Van Linden for a large sum. The track scene suited me well. Obviously sometimes some *arranging* went on, as witnessed by our transaction in Milan, but just like in the criteriums, the other team had to prove they could win. Whether we had finished 1st or 2nd in Milan our contract for the event was the same, as was our monthly salary. All we got was the pocket money that Gimondi had slipped us and that was much appreciated. The most important thing for me was that I felt in form and I demonstrated it straightaway by taking the Grand Prix of Laigueglia, the season's opener in Italy. During the winter it had been agreed that Flandria would send teams to ride in the Vuelta and the Giro, the latter because the interests of our co-sponsor, Latina, were primarily in Italy. There was to be no Tour de France for us, as riding the three major tours in one season was regarded as being beyond human possibilities for a team like ours whose riders were always expected to be playing an active role at the front. I know that the Spaniard José-Manuel Fuente once rode the Vuelta, the Giro and the Tour and afterwards had trouble with his health. As far as I know, the only rider to manage it successfully was Raphael Geminiani, who came 3rd in the

Giro and 6th in the Tour in 1956. Two years later he attempted the same mammoth task, but after finishing 5th in both the Vuelta and the Giro, he was unable to even finish the Tour of Switzerland. To me that says it all.

That season final victory was to be mine in both Paris-Nice and the Catalan Week. It was then that the rumour started going around that a number of riders had been found guilty of drug use during Paris-Nice. Ivan Sonck mentioned this on on the BRT television news and, without direct reference, linked my name with the affair by showing a photograph of me on the screen while the report was being read. I felt that this was a sordid insinuation and started proceedings against him for defamation of character.

Stress before important races was always a big thing with me. Anyone who doesn't know what it feels like would find it impossible to imagine how much torment it can create. To illustrate the point I'd like to tell you how I spent the day before the 1977 Tour of Flanders.

In the morning I said to my wife, "Will you bring my best suit with you to Meerbeke tomorrow for the reception because there's only going to be one winner today, and that's me."

When Carine heard me say that she knew it was too late. The past had taught her that when I made a prediction like that it often came true. However, My self-confidence quickly turned into highly charged nervousness when I noticed that all the newspapers had me down as the hot favourite.

In the afternoon the physio Jef Dhondt was to come and collect me so that we could set off for Flandria's team hotel in Sint-Niklaas. Once we'd had our midday meal, I didn't know what to do with myself while waiting for him. My nerves were stretched to the limit and I paced up and down the room. I was soon no longer in control of myself. While Carine was in another room getting my clothes ready, I started reacting to the restlessness which had taken over me in a very peculiar way. I took the cakes which my wife had bought for a visit she was expecting from her brother Rik and his family and stuck slices of tomatoes and other vegetables into them, piled them up and eventually I ended up throwing them at the walls of the room.

Suddenly, Carine realised what I was doing.

"Freddy! Have you gone mad?" she cried out in terror.

I calmed down and fortunately my brother Mario came and went off to the baker's to get some more cakes. By the time Carine's brother Rik, his wife Rita and their daughter Brigit arrived, you would have thought there was nothing wrong with me.

"Do you want some cognac with your coffee, Rik?" asked Carine.

"Yes please," Rik answered.

"You've forgotten to ask me," I said.

Everyone looked at me in amazement.

"But Freddy, you're riding in the Tour of Flanders tomorrow," said Carine, trying to point out how stupid my remark was.

"I'm still going to have a whisky anyway!" I maintained.

Carine came to the conclusion that I was beyond reasoning with and poured me a glass.

We talked about this and that until I suddenly said, "I want another whisky."

Only then did Carine really start to panic. She was thinking, 'If he really wants to win the Tour of Flanders tomorrow,' but she filled my glass again, realising that she couldn't change my mind for me.

As the minutes passed, I became more nervous, mainly because Jef Dhondt hadn't turned up when he was supposed to.

Now at her wit's end, Carine phoned him, "Jef, it's about time you were here. Freddy's become totally uncontrollable."

It wasn't until I was finally sitting in Jef's car that I calmed down.

Despite the previous day's odd behaviour, the Tour of Flanders ran its due course. Merckx made an early offensive but it didn't come off and De Vlaeminck and I got up to him. De Vlaeminck had a puncture but still managed to get back to us after a furious chase and it was Merckx who lost contact with us. On the Koppenberg, which was included in the circuit for the first time that year, many riders were due to change bikes as they had attached gears on their back wheels especially for the notorious climb and they wouldn't need them afterwards. These new bikes were only allowed to come from the team car. I was the first onto my second bike which was handed to me by somebody along the side of the road and I attacked immediately. Jos Fabri, who was then the chairman of the national sport committee of the BWB, drove up alongside me and accused me of not changing bikes according to the race rules. He didn't throw me out of the race there and then though, for the simple reason that he wanted to keep it a spectacle for the television cameras. Yes indeed, the whole situation was a *spectacle*. I towed Roger through the entire closing stages as he himself wouldn't do any lead work. With one and a half kilometres to go, the BWB came up to me to tell me that I would be allowed to take part in the sprint. However it could hardly be termed a sprint and De Vlaeminck won while I had to settle for 2nd place. Not for long, however. The race officials decided that I was to be disqualified and my name was wiped from the result. After all these years, if anyone can make any sense of the logic the BWB applied in that year's Tour of Flanders, they are welcome to come and explain it to me.

Four days later I avenged that costly shambles with victory in the Flèche Wallonne. It was without doubt one of the most satisfying wins in my whole career as I finished in Verviers on my own with a lead of more than four minutes. Yet even this victory was taken away from me. It appears that the substance *Stimul* could now be identified at dope controls. Once again the BWB demonstrated the same hypocrisy as in the 1974 season and left the riders alone for several weeks before unexpectedly lashing out with a long list of positive cases. In actual fact *Stimul* was a fairly harmless substance which affected the central nervous system. Everyone in the peloton took it and even Merckx was one of those who was caught. In Italy, however, they were aware of the fact that 'Stimul' was on the list of banned substances and that explains why Moser, who had finished 2nd behind me in the Flèche Wallonne, was eventually declared the winner.

A meeting for the Belgian riders was held at the Holiday Inn in Ghent to look into what measures we could take to get back at the BWB. Later we flew to Milan for discussions with our Italian counterparts. The sponsors were also unhappy and backed us all the way. Merckx, Gimondi, De Vlaeminck, they were all there in Milan but De Vlaeminck ruined the solidarity in pursuit of his own self-interest.

"I haven't been found positive so the whole business really isn't any of my concern," was his excuse.

It was a cowardly trick and because of him the unity was lost and no concrete action was ever taken.

Whenever De Vlaeminck could get something out of a situation for himself he would. The agreement which was made between us in the Hotel Thermal in Chaudfontaine after the Tour of Belgium in 1977 is the most striking example of that. De Vlaeminck and I both signed the contract [which is reproduced on page 89.]

The agreement was drawn up in the presence of De Vlaeminck, Lomme Driessens (whose idea it was), manager Firmin Verhelst and me. Verhelst was the indispensible neutral observer, cycling's notary as it were, and the person who was to guarantee the observance of the conditions of the contract. If either of us breached it he could impose sanctions when the contracts for criteriums were being drawn up.

Deals between riders have always taken place but usually they are only verbal. Perhaps in that hotel in Chaudfontaine it was the very first time in the history of the sport that an agreement between two riders was set down on paper so clearly beforehand. The average cycling fan will more than likely find this difficult to comprehend. I will simply repeat what I said earlier in this book – we were *professional* riders, with the stress on professional. You could call the pact between De Vlaeminck and me an *inter-professional* agreement. I didn't have to account to the average cycling fan for the fact that I wanted to earn as much as I could. Later on, when I was in financial trouble, I never saw this average cycling fan standing at my door with a bag of money.

Anyway, no matter what you put down on paper, you still don't have the money in your hand and that was certainly the case with the 1977 contract. Roger De Vlaeminck actually won Paris-Roubaix that year, ahead of Willy Teirlinck and me, but in Liège-Bastogne-Liège, Bernard Hinault prevented the completion of our contract while De Vlaeminck came 4th and I had to settle for 5th place. Then when the national championship in Yvoir arrived, things were totally different to the way they were planned, because of my fall during the Tour of Italy.

C O N T R A C T

The following contract has been drawn up between the riders Freddy Maertens and Roger De Vlaeminck.

1 - Roger De Vlaeminck pledges to ride in Paris-Roubaix on 17th April 1977 completely in the services of Freddy Maertens,

2 - Freddy Maertens pledges, in return, to ride in Liège-Bastogne-Liège on 24th April 1977 and also in the National Championship on 26th June 1977 completely in the service of Roger De Vlaeminck.

Read and approved   Read and approved
Fr. Maertens   Rog. De Vlaeminck

14th April 1977   14th April 1977

(signature)   (signature)

In the event of circumstances dictating that Freddy Maertens cannot win Paris-Roubaix, the Flandria team will ride in the service of Roger De Vlaeminck in Paris-Roubaix

Roger De Vlaeminck would then in that event ride in the service of Freddy Maertens in Liège-Bastogne-Liège and the National Championship.

Freddy Maertens   Roger De Vlaeminck

(signature)   (signature)

15 'Thick Lips'

During the early part of 1977 Carine and I regularly received threatening letters. While I was riding Paris-Nice, Carine even received a shotgun bullet through the letterbox. In the accompanying letter it said that during the course of Paris-Nice I would be shot dead by a bullet like this one. The police superintendent at Middelkerke began a thorough investigation but it was never established where it came from. The person who sent it was just as likely to have been a psychopath as a member of cycling's anti-Maertens brigade. Over the next few days Carine was very frightened and fortunately, as she always did when I was staying abroad, she went to stay wih my parents. Personally speaking, I wasn't too put out by the threat, but at the same time I wasn't completely relaxed.

Every night I would say to myself, "That's another stage where nothing terrible has happened."

We had bought some land on which we were to have a villa built (we moved into it at the end of 1977) and we drove a Mercedes. Perhaps that made certain people who were aware of my humble social background jealous, and that was the reason for the threatening and abusive letters we received. Why shouldn't I have improved my status, however, when I had been given the chance? I hadn't stolen the money but had simply earned it through hard work.

Every so often we had to change our telephone number. We had two numbers, one of which was generally known and one which was a private number. We only gave the private one to certain people with the specific request that they keep it to themselves, however, as is the case with private numbers, in the end everybody knew it. Whenever Driessens rang me, the arrangement was that he would first let it ring three times then hang up before immediately ringing back – that way I knew who it was.

Riders always seem to find it difficult being accepted in the area where they live, especially near the Belgian coast where there is a strong sense of envy. In 1975 I had signed a contract for a meeting at the Sport Palace in Ghent and on the very same day a race was organised in Lombardsijde. I didn't start in either of the races for the simple reason that I was ill. However, people thought that I had taken the easy way out, especially when Oscar Daemers who had organised the Ghent meeting, told journalists that I simply hadn't turned up. It seemed everybody was allowed to be sick except Freddy Maertens.

The first time public opinion had turned against me was after the famous world championship in Barcelona in 1973. Due to my heavy fall two days later in the criterium at Brasschaat I was unable to ride anywhere else at the end of that season, making it impossible for me to give my version of events in answer to Merckx' explanation of what happened on the Montjuich circuit. When did I ever get the chance to talk to journalists so that my case could be heard? Whenever I did get into the papers I was often shown in a negative light. For instance, on Friday 9th January 1976 a photograph appeared in the newspaper *Het Nieuwsblad* which annoyed Merckx and De Vlaeminck. While a journalist and photographer were at my house to see me, I returned home from a hunt and, like always, the first thing I did was to take my quarry out of the car and hang it in the garage.

"Let me take a photo of you with the game you've caught," suggested the photographer. "It will make a change from the customary photo of a rider and his bike."

Together with Carine I went outside with him, put my boots back on and posed for the camera with a hare in each hand. When the photo appeared later in the paper, the caption underneath read, *'Are these two Merckx and De Vlaeminck?'* I hadn't said anything at all like that, but Merckx and De Vlaeminck took it badly for a long time afterwards.

I was often booed but that honestly didn't bother me. At least it caused some atmosphere and it had the opposite effect to that intended by spurring me on to perform even better and so shut the mouths of the critics.

"Thick lips!" they used to shout.

OK, so I have got thick lips, I should know. It didn't bother me if they wanted to point it out to me, just as long as they didn't hit me with sticks. Even that happened once as I crossed the line in the national championship at Mettet. It turned out to be a fanatical Merckx supporter who wanted to put his placard to good use.

If it goes no further than booing though, it doesn't affect me.

Sometimes I even gestured to the person in question that he should give it some more. At other times, during the warming up, if someone in the crowd shouted *'Thick lips'* to me, I would nonchalently turn round and answer, 'Friend, you don't look like mother's finest to me either.' Sometimes I would turn the joke around and say, in a serious voice, 'If you can ride a bike as well as you can make smart comments, take this one, I'll just watch.' People like that who wanted to play the joker but who didn't expect any reaction tended to slink away somewhere, as there were nearly always people around them who would say, 'Well done Freddy, you do right to put him in his place.'

Whenever I'm deep in concentration, I have a rather sour looking face, and that meant that people tended to get the wrong impression of me. Often somebody who had met me would say, 'You're not at all the arrogant person I imagined you would be.' I think they are right as I don't have a difficult character. Before a race started, I was always totally engaged in thinking about the race and this made me look severe. Nevertheless, I've never failed to give my autograph when I've been asked. In fact, that was something I liked to do, especially for children and old people. I'd rather have signed too many autographs than never be seen by my fans. Sometimes, on an evening while watching television, I'd sign piles of photographs which were then sent to Commandant Lierman who answered my fan mail. This wasn't enough to satisfy the really *keen* ones though. They wanted you to sign your autograph in their presence so that they could be sure it was your signature and not a stamp.

It was good for cycling that you had fanatical supporters and opponents. It helped get things going. In those days ten thousand spectators used to come and watch the criterium at Moorslede, yet now it has been scrapped through lack of interest. The supporters always used to arrive a couple of hours before the start to see the stars arrive. Riders like Merckx, De Vlaeminck, Godefroot and Verbeeck stayed in the foreground of the sport for the whole year, while most riders nowadays only *peak* in a few important races a season. Everything has become less spicy.

No, I'm afraid there just aren't any really *daring* riders around any more.

16   Breaking Point

Mugello, Saturday 28th May 1977. Little did I realise, as I was winning my 7th stage in the Giro that morning, that this was to be the day that would bring about a complete turnabout in my career. In the afternoon a stage involving fifteen laps of the local motor-racing circuit was scheduled. The wind was coming from a different direction than in the morning, so I realised I was going to have to adapt my sprint tactics and definitely not to start it too early. The general feeling going around the tour caravan was that in the following day's time trial from Lucca to Pisa, which was just the right distance for me, I would take the pink jersey back from Francesco Moser.

The sprint in Mugello, however, dictated that things would be different. It began like any other sprint with Michel Pollentier taking on the preparation and Marc Demeyer towing me along in the final kilometre. All of a sudden, Rik Van Linden went out in front with a side wind against us. When I got up to him and was about to pass, he caught me with his elbow.

Sprinting, by definition, holds risks, everyone knows that. Carine was scared to death to watch any sprint in which I was involved on the television. As a rider though, if you are afraid, you will come off worst and you'd best be advised to slam your brakes on. It is vital to be able to steer your bike skilfully. In the Tour of Italy, a sprint actually begins 60 kilometres from the finish, as that's when the pace increases and you have to choose your place in the group.

Because of Van Linden's manoeuvre (which video recordings clearly show), our bikes wobbled into each other. Marino Basso won, and while I was lying there unconscious Van Linden managed to stumble over the line after the crash. I was immediately rushed to the rather primitive hospital in Lucca, which with all its white walls looked like a monastery. The first thing I was able to hear while in there was that if I didn't pass water within the next half hour, according to the dope control rules, I would have to be found positive. Even in my badly battered state, I still managed to do it. Only then could the medical staff begin to deal with the injuries all over my body. My wounds were stitched in several places, but the most serious appeared to be my right wrist which was diagnosed as broken, meaning my lower arm needed to be put in plaster.

After the race Driessens lodged a complaint against Van Linden for illegal sprinting and the race officials upheld it by issuing a fine and a five minute time penalty. Van Linden's directeur sportif, Gimondi was very unhappy about it and he threatened to pull his whole team out of the Giro. Because our co-sponsors had insured me for BF 10 million they wanted to begin court proceedings later in Belgium, but eventually the idea was dropped.

After I had been patched up in the hospital in Lucca they allowed me to return to the hotel where our team was staying. I rode on the rollers for half an hour straightaway to get the stiffness out of my body but the results were disappointing. This made me realise that it would probably be best if I didn't start the following day.

That made Pollentier and Demeyer want the whole Flandria team to drop out of the tour.

"No," said Lomme. "One *dead man* doesn't mean that life on earth stops."

Demeyer was annoyed with Lomme's lack of tact that day. Indeed, I think I would have found a more subtle way of convincing the lads that they shouldn't quit the Giro for me.

After a sleepless night, the doctor came the next morning to put another type of plaster on my arm to enable me to grip my handlebars. I decided to familiarise myself with the time trial route from Lucca to Pisa on my racing bike. That removed any doubts that I still had. I realised it was hopeless as I just couldn't get enough strength into controlling the handlebars.

In spite of this Lomme tried to convince me to give it a go. "It will be all right," he tried to reassure me. The organiser of the Giro, Torriani, however, could see things more objectively and stated that he could understand my decision.

My team-mates once again suggested that we should all go home to Belgium together, and there was even talk that we should ride in the Tour de France instead, even though it wasn't in our original programme for the season. That would have been out of the question, though, as having ridden in the classics, the Vuelta and the Giro, everyone had already had such a demanding season that we would have hardly been able to put a team together that had any strength left. I therefore pointed out to the rest of the team that it would be better if they stayed, especially in view of the fact that Michel was high up in the classification and that Marc could maybe win a stage. I honestly have to admit that at that point, the possibility that Michel would finish in the pink jersey hadn't crossed my mind. But had it crossed anybody's?

On that day I followed the time trial in Torriani's car behind Moser. Later, Torriani addressed the crowd from the podium in Pisa and I was given a heart-warming round of applause as a farewell. My suitcases and bike were put into a Lada and were taken, with me, the couple of hundred kilometres to Milan airport.

"Your ticket will be waiting for you there," Lomme had promised.

However, when I arrived there, there was no sign of any reservation having been made. There I was, the reigning world champion, left to my own devices, completely alone with my cases and bike. At that moment I realised for the first time ever how transient fame is.

Luckily I had some Eurocheques with me so I was able to pay for a ticket. I couldn't catch the first two planes and I was forced to wait until 11 o'clock that evening for the final flight. It arrived at Zaventem not long after midnight and Carine and her friend Christa came to collect me in the car. Fortunately there weren't any journalists around. I'd told Carine on the telephone not to tell anyone exactly when I would be arriving back.

Once at home I followed the rest of the Giro on television and saw Michel claim the pink jersey. That made me really happy and, contrary to what was written about me later, did not cause me any pain. I was really happy for him in his hour of success, just like I was for Marc with his two stage wins.

On the final day I flew to Milan with Paul Claeys. Before the start of the final stage I congratulated Michel on his overall victory and the rest of my team-mates on their sterling work.

"Just one final push, then you'll be able to go home!" I said, encouraging them.

Suddenly Lomme came up to me.

"What are you doing here?" he said agitatedly. "You haven't left anything behind here. The only reason you've come is to steal some of our publicity!"

That simply wasn't true as the only reason I had come was because Paul Claeys insisted I should. Claeys wasted no time in putting Driessens right on that score.

After the stage was over I paid for champagne for the whole team. Michel, however, was missing from the celebrations. After the final presentations Driessens had shunted him off to his car and driven him somewhere fifteen kilometres outside Milan. That was so typical of Lomme, he always wanted to be with the man of the moment. Paul Claeys was absolutely furious and the rest of the team didn't appreciate it very much, but it wasn't really Michel's fault. It was very rare that a rider could stop Lomme doing what he wanted to do.

At Lomme's request I took part in the Tour of Switzerland and this was, without doubt, the biggest blunder I ever made in my sporting career. If my performances in 1978 and 1979 weren't up to scratch, the origins can be traced back to this misadventure. As a result of the plaster cast on my right arm I had to sit slightly sideways on my saddle and my back was overburdened on one side. As if it wasn't enough that my arm hadn't healed sufficiently, I ended up struggling with my back. Nevertheless, I won the first stage, but over the next few days I suffered terrible pain. In the final time trial at Ellretikon I was unable to start. Fortunately for Flandria, Michel Pollentier was the overall winner here as well. Despite his double success I didn't feel that my team leadership was under threat, but it did disturb me that he was beginning to receive offers from other teams. He remained level-headed though, and his relationship with me didn't change. Nonetheless, I was still worried that he might not be by my side when the following season commenced.

On the days leading up to the national championship at Yvoir, Michel claimed in interviews that he would be riding in my service completely during the championship race. This was in fact a tactic to mislead all our rivals as I knew full well that I didn't stand a chance of winning on the Yvoir circuit. Pollentier's words were deliberately intended to make the others keep an eye on me. When Michel attacked a few circuits from the finish they all thought that his intention was to make it easier for me at the end and he had, therefore, been forced to take the initiative. They had, however, made a serious miscalculation. Michel built up a bigger and bigger lead and in the end he was so far in front that I could afford to retire before the finish.

It was, therefore, the very time that I was struggling that Michel was experiencing one high point after another. I consoled myself with the thought that one day all my physical problems would be behind me and everything would go back to how it had been before. For the time being all I could do was keep hoping and trust that everything would turn out all right. When Michel extended his contract with Flandria, it was at least one piece of reassuring encouragement.

On July 13th 1977, I fought out a challenge in Amiens with the racehorse, Fakir du Vivier, belonging to the French film star, Alain Delon. Lomme had organised this head to head confrontation. I received BF 120,000 to start plus another BF 50,000 from the bookmakers if I lost! This I did by three-tenths of a second, or to put it in horse-racing terminology, by a nose.

The horse was given the inside track of the racecourse and next to that they rolled the cinders smooth for me over the whole 1,000 metre distance. There was a massive crowd for this strange spectacle and the most that was expected of me was that I would make a go of it. After a flying start, I sheltered from the wind by staying tucked in just behind the sulky with the jockey. In the final straight I changed into my 53x12 gear and came up alongside Fakir du Vivier and then made sure that he made the finishing line first by a whisker. There was talk of a revenge race being organised at the racecourse at either Sterrebeek or Kuurne but the BWB forbade it. This same ruling body demanded that they inspect my contract for Amiens afterwards. According to them, I should have asked for their permission to take part in this one-off event. What we did at the time was draw up a false contract showing a ficticious amount. On the strength of that, the good gentlemen, in their wisdom, decided to hold back BF 7,000 of this total in the form of a fine, for the sake of more honour and glory for the BWB funds.

Two days before the world championships in the little town of San Cristobal in Venezuela, Michel was forced to swerve to avoid a hole in the road during a practice ride and a car ran in to him. He ended up with a broken collarbone as a result. That meant only Marc Demeyer and Herman Beyssens were left from the Flandria team to lend me support in the battle for the title. The evening before the title race the gathering of the Belgian team once again turned into the usual rumpus. Merckx and Godefroot especially found Driessens' pushiness difficult to take and I ended up paying the price.

I rode the whole race on the offensive, countering any attacks by riders from other countries and was feeling every bit as strong as I did in Ostuni. Bitossi attacked and I managed to stay with him until we were eventually caught. Then Thurau saw his chance and Moser went with him. I gave everything I had in the chase and asked Godefroot to help me but he said he had nothing more left in him. At the same time though, he was riding smoothly with his hands on the top of his handlebars. The truth was that he simply didn't *want* to do his share of the work. Furious because of this lack of support, I retired from the race during the final circuit, even though 3rd place was within my reach. I wasn't interested in it, though. I gave the same explanation to the BWB as Godefroot had given me: *I couldn't do any more.*

In San Cristobal I once more announced that I would be having a crack at the world hour record in Mexico City. In the back of my mind I knew it was a case of now or never. However, just like twelve months earlier, Paul Claeys threw the idea out. Eddy Merckx once said in an interview that his world hour record had cost him a couple of years of his career. If that is correct there is no point in me shedding any tears about never having had the opportunity to break the record.

After the world championship I won the Tour of Catalonia, but in the Autumn classics I was unable to do anything special. In Paris-Brussels I fell and my back trouble returned. To make matters worse, Carine was also having trouble with her health and had to spend some time in hospital. Lomme insisted I should ride the Grand Prix des Nations even though it was perfectly obvious to me that I had no chance in this time trial event. The outcome was that I had to concede several minutes to Hinault. The Tour of Lombardy brought no points for me for the Super Prestige, yet despite my poor end of season results and my disqualifications in both the Tour of Flanders and the Flèche Wallonne earlier in the season, for the second successive year I was the winner of this competition which rewarded consistency. This was in no small part due to my victory in the Tour of Spain in which I had won no fewer than 13 stages.

In the last race I started in 1977, an 80 kilometre criterium in Longchamps, I won again. This brought my total number of victories for the season to 53, only one less than in 1976. If it hadn't been for my fall in Mugello my own record would have stood for scarcely one year.

Driessens was sacked by Flandria at the end of the 1977 season. Marc Demeyer especially wanted him out. He and Michel had only signed for one more year but I was contracted for another two. I took their side against Lomme and Paul Claeys granted our demand without much resistance. This was not least because Driessens was becoming increasingly self-opinionated as time went on. For instance, on one occasion when Paul Claeys was standing waiting to ride a few circuits in Driessens' car during the national championships in Yvoir, Lomme said, "No profiteers in my car!" and just left his own boss standing where he was. Another time was when co-sponsor Valère Veldeman appeared at the Giro to wish Michel Pollentier luck in defending his pink jersey and was told by Lomme, "We never see you at any other time so I don't want you getting under our feet now."

The task of taking over from Driessens fell to Fred De Bruyne who wanted to swap his job as a television commentator for one as a directeur sportif no matter what it cost. The firm thought it would be great for publicity to have a well known face attracting attention in the team car. Fred, in turn, saw us as the ideal partners to help him make a successful return to the peloton after his own cycling career.

He would soon regret it – and so would we.

17   Good Manners

Fred De Bruyne, who had been out of cycling for such a long time, came to my house regularly in the winter of 1977-78 and we would talk for hours. I tried to give him a thorough re-introduction to the current scene. It also has to be said that Fred had ambition. One of his greatest *ambitions* was to teach good table manners to the Flandria team riders and make them into gentlemen. Sometimes, however, I wondered who needed a lesson in good breeding the most – the pupils or the master himself.

For instance, there was the day Fred and his wife Lydië arrived unexpectedly at our house after a visit to the firm in Zedelgem, dressed to the nines.

"It's my wife's birthday today and I'd like to invite you both to come and eat with us somewhere," Fred enthusiastically announced as soon as he was inside.

Carine and I replied by saying how nice it was of them to suggest it but that we had already cooked a meal and that it would be perhaps better to accept the invitation on another occasion.

"No," insisted Fred. "You're coming with us this minute."

We allowed ourselves to be persuaded.

"Do you know a nice restaurant around here?" asked Fred. "One that's of a high quality."

We suggested 't Hoeveke in Oostduinkerke, a place to which we had often taken friends in the past.

Once there, Fred ordered an extensive menu comprising champagne as an aperitif, dishes accompanied by red wine and white wine, more champagne and finally coffee with cake and pousse-café.

It was a delicious meal, but in the meantime it was getting late and I noticed that the owner wanted to close up. I wondered when Fred was eventually going to pay but he seemed to have all the time in the world. Gradually, Carine started looking at me inquisitively and made a move to get her chequebook from her handbag. I shook my head, though, to let her know that she shouldn't.

After another half an hour of chit-chat I could also see that Fred had lost any thoughts about paying.

"Can I have the bill please?" I asked the restaurant owner.

Carine gave me a cheque and I filled in the amount.

"Listen, the last bottle of champagne is on me," chipped in Fred generously.

"Forget it." I said grumpily. "I'll pay for *everything.*"

It was Carine and I who had been invited, but when it came down to it we had to fork out more than BF 12,000.

Lomme Driessens had a similar thing happen to him with Fred during the 1978 Tour de France. One evening they had to go somewhere together. It had been a stiflingly hot day and Fred suggested they should go and have a bottle of wine on a terrace bar.

When the bottle was empty, Lomme said, 'Now it's my turn to get one.'

"No," answered Fred. "We'll order another bottle but I'll pay for it."

When they had finished that one Lomme repeated, "The next one's on me."

"I won't hear of it," insisted Fred emphatically.

At a certain moment he went to the toilet and when he came back he said in a disconcerted voice, "Guillaume, I hope you have some French money on you as I seem to have forgotten my wallet."

Lomme had no alternative but to pay for the three bottles.

A third illustration of Fred's etiquette was when, before the start of the season, we both had an appointment at the Volvo factory concerning the team cars we would be getting. I called at Fred's first and when we left his house together his wife asked me, "Will you be eating here later?"

"I don't know," I answered. "I don't think it will take that long and if it doesn't I'll go straight back to Westende."

However, our discussions at the Volvo factory did last longer than expected. When we arrived back at Fred's house, Lydië opened the front door and welcomed me with the words, "Oh, I haven't prepared anything for you to eat."

All of these instances are only meant to show how appropriate it was that Fred should be the person to teach riders their table manners.

Anyway, Fred fell totally short of what was needed to be a directeur sportif. In the Tour de France he usually only got back to the hotel late on, meaning he could never get up on time in the morning. We were often already in our racing gear when his lordship came downstairs, after which he would quickly have a cup of coffee and shoot off to the car. Then there wouldn't be enough petrol in the car and the team personnel would have to pay for it. That was the big difference with Lomme, who was always spot on when it came to details in the organisation.

Sometimes Fred made the mechanic drive the team car while he had a nap, or he would listen to music instead of the tour radio. You can imagine what sort of situation that would have led to if one of us had suffered a puncture. When that happened, other directeurs sportifs had to give him a signal to let him know that one of his riders needed him.

An incident with Marc Demeyer at the Hotel Cheval Blanc in St-Etienne showed just how far dissatisfaction among the riders had escalated. The Flandria team bus (in which were a massage table and a refrigerator) which followed us around the Tour had developed a faulty door and the Belgian manufacturers Desot were sending two men to come and repair it. They arrived at the hotel about three-quarters of an hour before we were due to have our evening meal.

"Would you like a drink?" asked Fred.

"Yes please," they answered.

When their glasses were empty Fred said, "Why don't you two stay and eat with us."

"We'd rather not," one of them said. "We'd prefer it if you'd show us exactly what's wrong with the bus first please, because as soon as we've finished here we have to set off for a repair in Lyon."

"My riders and I are going to eat first," decided Fred and he nervously left the two technicians at the bar.

"Come on Fred, go with them so they can make a start on the work," said Marc Demeyer who was sitting directly across the table from De Bruyne. Fred, however, remained unrelenting.

A little later Marc tried again: "Fred, don't you realise the repairmen are in a hurry?"

"For God's sake," Fred called out. "Who's the boss here – you or me."

Oh dear, it would have been better if he had held those words back.

Muscleman Demeyer stretched one hand across the table and grabbed De Bruyne by the throat and then with one heave sent him flying into the corner of the room, where he landed between some chairs.

"More! More! More!" we all chanted.

Spurred on by our encouragement, Marc went up to De Bruyne and thumped him again.

Fred meekly cried, "Please Marc, stop it."

Once again though, we all shouted "More! More! More!"

Members of another team were in the same dining room and they made sure the news spread rapidly around the whole tour caravan.

The next day, Fred wisely kept himself in the background.

We weren't to know in January that Fred would turn out to be a total failure as a team manager. Michel Pollentier received another lucrative offer from Italy but didn't succumb to temptation because of the improved contract he had been awarded by Flandria the year before. At the end of the month he won the Two Days of Majorca. The season also started brightly for me when I won a stage in the same meeting followed by victories in Seillans-Draguignan and Het Volk. Fred wept when I took the honours in Belgium's season opener and it wasn't just for show. He is certainly a sensitive person who allows his emotions free reign.

In the Amstel Gold Race Jan Raas rode away to victory on his own, while in the sprint for second place I had to give way to Moser and Zoetemelk.

This led me to the conclusion that I had lost some speed. That may have been true to a certain extent – I did indeed win fewer stages in the Tour de France that year – but another explanation was that I definitely had to do more work for myself during races in 1978. First and foremost this was due to a lack of organisation by De Bruyne, and secondly there were still rumours going round the peloton that Michel Pollentier would definitely be leader of another team the following season. The fact that a number of riders might be going with him led to a certain amount of discord in the team.

On Saturday 1st April, I was told to go out and win the E3 Race at Harelbeke where co-sponsor Pierre Lano, who was getting married on that day, lived. He wasn't one of my greatest friends, though. When the team presentation took place at his company headquarters he really tore into Pollentier, Demeyer and me because we had supposedly arrived late. With Paul Claeys' permission, we had gone on a massive training ride that morning and we arrived in plenty of time for the photo session. However, Lano didn't think so and he gave us a real mouthful, backed up by Fred De Bruyne, when we showed up.

Anyway, on that Saturday, 1st April, all of the Flandria team riders stood outside the church in Hulste with a wheel in our hands forming a guard of honour before the start of the E3 Race. Pierre Lano had promised me BF 80,000 if I could provide him with the victory he wanted as a wedding present. I managed it by giving BF 40,000 of it to Jan Raas with whom I had escaped somewhere near the Old Kwaremont. However, when I went to collect the BF 80,000 I had been promised by Lano, it was only after a great deal of argument on both sides that I received it.

In the crucial week in April I finished 8th in the Tour of Flanders, 9th in Ghent-Wevelgem and 4th in Paris-Roubaix. In the 'Hell of the North,' four of us were out in front: Raas, Moser, De Vlaeminck and me. Moser and De Vlaeminck took turns to attack and on each occasion I brought them back – something that was made more difficult by the fact that Raas had shot his bolt and could offer no help. Moser knew that if he wanted to get away on his own he would have to have a word with me. This he did, and when he tried to get away for the umpteenth time I didn't respond.

"Go and get after him!" De Vlaeminck cursed.

Both he and Moser knew that they would both be riding for Sanson the following season and because of that they worked together to a degree. De Vlaeminck, however, would have liked to have justified his title of *Monsieur Paris-Roubaix*. Unlike Moser though, he decided he didn't need to seek my counsel and therefore he simply had to accept the consequences.

In Liège-Bastogne-Liège I took 9th place. Here, Fred De Bruyne once again demonstrated his *qualities* as a directeur sportif. While I was struggling with a puncture he flew past to get tucked in behind Pollentier and Bruyère, even though there was absolutely no need to. Our mechanic, Freddy Heydens, was forced to ride back to me, in the opposite direction to the race, on my reserve bike.

According to some people the reason I didn't add a classic to my honours list in 1978 was my excessive use of the big gears during the previous two seasons. I was generally regarded as the leading advocate of big gears and indeed it's true that I would rather descend with a 54x12 than a 52x13 for example, because I found that this put less strain on my heart. Before our day nobody used these gears and it was Pollentier, Demeyer and I who initiated the *twelve* into the peloton, although it wasn't long before others followed.

In normal circumstances I used a 52x12 gear. Driessens always wanted his say in our choice of gears but actually he knew nothing about it. He once even claimed to journalists that I rode time trials with a 55x12. Didn't he realise exactly what that would involve? The only time I used a 55x12 (in fact it was a 55x11) was in the Ganshoren-Meulebeke Race which was behind a derny.

Sometimes Driessens nagged me so much about which cogs I was going to be using the following day that I got so fed up that I would end up agreeing with him just so that he would shut up. Behind his back, however, I did it the way I wanted and the mechanics did what I asked them to do.

"You see. I was right," Lomme would boast when I won another time trial in this way.

In my opinion, a rider doesn't need to have a particular physique to able to use a big gear. There was a great difference in the way Pollentier and I were built, yet we both rode with the same gears. It is also worth pointing out that Michel, Marc and I never had any trouble with tendinitis.

I'm sure that if the big gear had existed in Coppi's time, he would also have used it. Like the disc wheel, it is simply an evolution in cycling which has helped improve performances and those who refuse to go along with new trends will always be left on the side-lines.

18 The Crossroads

I was the overall victor in the Dunkirk Four Days for the fourth time in early May 1978. This was the month when Eddy Merckx suddenly announced his retirement from professional cycling. It was unexpected and yet, at the same time, it was not. He had been struggling all season and had come to the conclusion that his best days were behind him.

The best days of the Flandria team of old were also over, especially with the knowledge that Michel Pollentier would be riding in another team's colours the following season. In an interview with the Belgian magazine *Panorama*, Fred once said: *"My experience is that there is a certain rivalry between Demeyer and Pollentier in the shadow of Maertens. They are battling to see who could get the closest to Freddy, striving to be the best servant. Demeyer won Paris-Roubaix and Paris-Brussels and felt he was the best but then along came Pollentier and won the Tour of Italy, the Tour of Switzerland and the National Championships. Maertens played them off against each other: one day he was close to one of them, the next day the other.'*

Fred exaggerates when he uses the term 'servant' but it was right that a rivalry was being played out by Pollentier and Demeyer. When Michel received his improved contract at the end of 1977, we had to pull the wool over Marc's eyes. Two identical contracts were offered by Paul Claeys to Pollentier and Demeyer so that Marc would not be jealous. However, Pollentier had further talks with Paul Claeys two days later and that's when Michel signed his actual contract. Marc also wanted to take part in as many races as Michel, so, in 1977 for example, he had to be selected for the climbing event at Montjuich in Spain, even though he knew only too well that he wouldn't do anything. Marc, however, failed to take into account that he took part in track meetings during the winter while Michel only took part in cyclo-cross events as preparation for the road season.

As Fred De Bruyne had lost all of his authority, I thought it would be a good idea to bring in Briek Schotte again as directeur sportif for the 1978 Tour de France. We met each other again for the first time in ages at Ann Monseré's and discussed it there, though in the end the plan never came to fruition.

Before the Tour de France, there was still the National Championship at Vielsalm to come and it was agreed that Michel Pollentier would be helping me to win the title. However, when he suddenly attacked on a climb, De Vlaeminck and Godefroot did not respond.

"If you want to win, you'll have to go and chase him yourself," they challenged me mockingly.

That made me realise that Pollentier was *in league* with them. In this way he was able to retain the national jersey which he had won the year before in Yvoir and I was so furious that I didn't bother to fight out the sprint for a place on the podium. Just before the line I dismounted and went to the Flandria team bus. I can tell you that inside it there was some pretty strong language used that day as Marc Demeyer didn't hide his annoyance either. By the evening things had been partially smoothed over and we went for a meal with our partners to the restaurant at the Flandria Ranch in Torhout where we stayed until day break.

To this day, Michel still denies that he *stabbed me in the back* at Vielsalm and claims that he only won because De Vlaeminck and Godefroot were out to sabotage me that day. He is so insistent on this being the truth that I feel I must believe him.

The Tour de France prologue took place in the Dutch town of Leiden amid rather chaotic scenes. In the hall of the vegetable market where the starting signal was to be given, there were lots of advertising hoardings for which the Tour administration had received no money. The Tour director, Felix Lévitan, therefore decided to keep the prologue in purely for appearance's sake with the result not counting towards the overall classification. When Jan Raas won, however, he was allowed to start the following day in the yellow jersey, directly contradicting the official announcement that had been made the day before. Raas also won the first part of the second stage which finished in Sint-Willebrord after he had pushed himself off from the sturdy aerial on the car carrying the mobile television camera. I came second in that stage. In the second part of the stage, from Sint-Willebrord to Brussels, I had to swerve to avoid a motorcycle policeman during the sprint and was unable to get past Walter Planckaert.

The atmosphere within the Flandria team was already frosty and became more so as a result of my double misfortune. It was already known that Herman Beyssens and Roger Verschaeve were to be part of Pollentier's new team in 1979 and this suggested that I could no longer count on their support. I am not saying this to attach blame, but simply to make the reader aware that I had to fend for myself in this Tour a lot more than had been the case in the past. For his part, despite the fact that he was aiming for a high place in the classification, Michel put himself at my service during the final stretches of the flat stages to help me retain the green jersey. This paid dividends twice in three days: firstly in Maze-Montgeoffroy and later in Bordeaux.

Four days after the riders had taken strike action in Valence d'Agen, there was the stage to Alpe d'Huez on July 16th where Michel took the yellow jersey but was caught in the act of cheating at the dope control – an incident which will go down in the annals of cycling as *pee-history*.

I wasn't there to witness it myself, as I didn't have to report to the dope control that day.

When Michel came into the room he said, "I've been caught."

"What do you mean?" I asked.

"They took my clothes away and noticed I was cheating," he answered. Michel was devastated. I telephoned Jacques Goddet and asked him if some sort of arrangement couldn't be reached.

"No, the race commissaires will not revoke their decision," I was told.

Later on Michel's wife rang up, disenchanted and disgusted.

"Josiane, you must stand by your husband now more than ever," I said.

In the corridor dozens of journalists were trying to force their way in, but we kept everyone out and locked the door. Outside, the photographers were lining up with their zoom lenses in the hope of catching a glimpse of us.

Our co-sponsor, Valère Veldeman, who was on holiday in Fontainebleu at the time, had been following Pollentier's triumph on the radio and, together with his wife, had immediately jumped into his car to come and congratulate him. He was as happy as a lark when he arrived at our room and embraced Michel. He was obviously unaware of the drama that had unfolded.

"Mr and Mrs Veldeman, would you just like to come with me into the bathroom," I said, trying to bring them back down to earth.

108

Two pieces of action from the Four Days at Dunkirk in 1974.
(*above*) Maertens lying in third place as the bunch take a corner.
(*below*) Taking a left-hand corner ahead of Britain's Barry Hoban.
(*both John Coulson*)

Long-standing Flandria team-mate of Freddy's, here seen in action helping him to the green jersey in the 1976 Tour de France, was: Michel Pollentier,

Marc Demeyer, winner of that year's Paris-Roubaix (*both Photosport International*)

Walter Godefroot was a stalwart of the Flandria team during Maertens' first two seasons as a professional.

The arrival of Lomme Driessens as directeur sportif was the cue for Godefroot's departure. Over subsequent seasons Driessens was to be a major influence in Maertens' career. (*both Photosport International*)

Maertens, in the yellow jersey, here has time to adjust a toe strap on his way to winning the time trial at Le Touquet during his Tour de France debut in 1976. (*John Coulson*)

The 1977 classics saw Maertens in the rainbow jersey. Here he is seen during Paris-Roubaix with team-mate Pollentier. (*Photosport International*)

Wearing the green jersey as points leader in the 1978 Tour de France, Maertens is a source of attention to the media, when either signing on (*above*) or riding a time trial (*below*) (*both Photosport International*)

By the time the Tour caravan reached Alpe d'Huez in 1978, and most of the attention was focused on Michel Pollentier's successful, but ultimately ill-fated attempts to take the yellow jersey.

Several minutes later and Maertens climbs Alpe d'Huez, unaware at the time of the furore to surround the Flandria team later that same day. (*both Photosport International*)

(*above*) It was to be 1981 before Maertens was seen in the Tour de France again. The team jersey was again red, but this time - as a member of the Boule d'Or team - Sunair were the main sponsors during this event. (*below*) He was soon back in the green jersey, attracting the attention of the cycling public. (*both Photosport International*).

In 1982 Maertens was again in the rainbow jersey for Paris-Roubaix. Here he is in the thick of the action with, among others, Eddy Planckaert.

As his career drew to its close, Freddy was to be seen on a regular basis on the street circuits of Britain during the Kellogg's City Centre series, here at Manchester in 1986. (*both Photosport International*)

"There is a slight problem."

Taken totally aback and shattered by the news, they returned to Fontainebleu, not least because nobody had informed them downstairs. Indeed, this painful situation could have been avoided. That evening it was deathly quiet in our room. We did not discuss the reason why Michel had done what he had done. It had happened and there was no use in grumbling about it. When the evening meal arrived, I opened the door and stuck my foot in front of it to make sure no journalists could force their way in. I ate, but Michel hardly touched any of his food.

The following day was a rest day and so, to escape the inquisitive questions of the assembled journalists, I got out through the basement, sneaked into the car and drove to a place well away from the hotel so that I could go for a training stint on my bike.

Michel's greatest fear was how they would react to the affair in Belgium. As it turned out it went far better than he had hoped – they took his side. One reason was that they appreciated that he had admitted his guilt and hadn't tried to mislead anyone about what he had done. Another reason was that public opinion in Belgium also suspected that dope controls in the Tour de France operated double standards, something which I can only confirm from my own experience. The expressions of sympathy which came Michel's way in Belgium gave his morale a great lift. During his suspension, when he appeared at criteriums to give the start signal, it was not unusual for him to receive more applause than any of the riders.

During this time Pollentier and I rarely saw each other other than at these criteriums. In August he signed a professional contract with Armand Marlair to become the team-leader for the Splendor team in 1979. I've always regretted that Michel didn't let me know personally beforehand. We were both adults so wouldn't it have been possible to have talked to each other about it? We had been able to discuss things together for years, why couldn't we at that moment?

Later, Michel did come looking for me to act as a mediator with Paul Claeys so that he would let him leave. Claeys could see that it was useless to keep him against his wishes, as there would have been little chance of expecting top performances from him. He was also prepared to come to a settlement. At Splendor, Michel could earn three times as much as at Flandria and was therefore right in wanting to seize his opportunity. What wasn't so pleasant – and this was to become apparent at the end of the season – was that he would be taking several members of the Flandria team to his new employees: riders Sean Kelly, Herman Beyssens, Roger Verschaeve, Wim Myngheer, Lieven Malfait and Christian Dumont as well as mechanic, Freddy Heydens, and physios Jef Dhondt and Luc Landuyt.

The journalists, naturally, regarded the split between Pollentier and me as perfect material to fill their columns with and they put words into Michel's mouth about me and my private life which were so far fetched that it became impossible for me to believe that he had actually said them. At around that time I was also sometimes quoted in articles without ever having spoken to the journalist in question, even on the telephone.

Michel missed the world championship on the Nürburgring as a result of his suspension. When seven of us were taking up the chase after Hinault, I fell, thanks to Zoetemelk, and was forced to retire. In the closing stages, with two men at the front, Knetemann told Moser, who had dug in behind, that he was finished and would be happy with second place. However, in the sprint, his energy suddenly came flooding back. The Italian team almost lynched the bespectacled Dutchman that day.

During the months of October and November it appeared to the outside world as though I had vanished into thin air. In truth I was keeping well away from the press so that I wouldn't be confronted with questions concerning my relationship with Pollentier. Together with Carine, Marc Demeyer and his wife and Raoul Bouve and his wife, I stayed for two weeks at the ski-resort of Les Deux Alpes to enjoy the scenery and the cross-country skiing. At least I would be left in peace there and I could think about the future without any distractions.

In December, I appeared before the journalists once more, with Robert Sergooris, a man who had been handling my business affairs for several years, by my side. As was to become apparent later, to my detriment and embarrassment, it would be more accurate to say he handled *his* business affairs. In the meantime, he had also been appointed accountant for the Flandria Ranch, a concern at Torhout, in which Paul Claeys and I were business partners, and he was given the job of becoming business manager of the Flandria team. He was to demonstrate that he didn't have a clue about cycling the following season.

Amidst all the tribulations of the 1978 season, there was one event on which I could look back with a great deal of pride. On September 2nd my daughter Romy was born and this was without doubt the finest performance of my life.

19   Two Belgians in America

Part of the Flandria team for the 1979 season consisted of riders who had been transferred from Merckx's disbanded C & A team: Joseph Bruyère (whom I was counting on to take over Pollentier's role), Jos De Schoenmaecker, Ward Janssens and René Martens. The physio, Guillaume Michiels, was also part of the transfer deal. Jos Huysmans, who the year before was still riding in C & A's colours, was making his debut as directeur sportif with us. All of these old-guard Merckx riders made sure that the atmosphere in the Flandria ranks soon turned bad, not least by putting the idea into Marc Demeyer's head that he, and not me, deserved to be team-leader.

A plot was hatched against me during the training camp in the Côte d'Azure to bring my name into disrepute. One day, after group training, I was summoned to see Sergooris who was also there with us.

"How long have you been using amphetamines when you go training?" he asked me in the tone of an examining magistrate.

I had no idea what he was getting at.

"While you were all out, Guillaume Michiels asked the receptionist for the key to your room and found these ampoules in your rubbish bin," continued Sergooris.

"That's impossible," I assured him.

"Well what are these then," he answered and produced several used ampoules. It was only then that it sunk in what sort of game they had been playing with me and that it would be impossible for me to prove the accusation was false. At the same time all of this was going on I was perfectly aware that a number of other riders were definitely taking amphetamines in order to be able to burn me off in training, something they managed on a couple of occasions.

Indignant at this cowardly allegation, I took a plane home on my own. It was crystal clear to me that this was going to be an awful season. Sergooris informed Paul Claeys and Michiels gave the knife a further twist by letting *Mister Paul* know that he felt he should give me the friendly advice to give up cycling. The end would then have justified the means.

Before the training camp I was again struggling with my right wrist, the abiding consequence of my fall in Mugello during the Giro in 1977. I consulted several doctors and surgery appeared to be unavoidable, even though I was afraid of that option as I thought it would put the whole of the early season into jeopardy. At the end of January Professor Claessens and Dr Verhelst from Izegem carried out the operation at the Academy Hospital in Ghent. The *os lunatum* (moon-shaped bone) in my right wrist was cracked. During the operation the surgeons performed an extension by sawing through my ulna in a Z-shape and forcing it four millimetres apart and then inserting a plate with twelve screws between it. I still carry all of this around with me.

Know-it-alls put the fact that I still have trouble with the injury I received in Mugello down to an excessive use of cortisone, one of the side-effects of which is that the cartilage flakes off. Well, that is definitely not the real reason. The actual explanation is that in January 1979 – nearly two years after it had happened – Dr Verhelst was the first doctor to succeed in making the correct diagnosis. I am not claiming that I have never been administered cortisone in my career, but just that when I did, it was only when a doctor considered it necessary for my system; in other words, if the medical treatment justified it.

On March 11th I took part in my first race of the season, the Circuit of the Flemish Ardennes at Ichtegem. I rode it with my forearm in a leather sleeve which had been made especially to fit my arm, but I didn't make it to the finish. Six days later I started in Milan-San Remo, but at the feeding post at Savonna I clambered into the team-car. I was well below the level of fitness required but, more than that, my morale was at a low ebb. Afterwards I was criticised for wanting to ride in Milan-San Remo but what else was I supposed to do – sit at home? At least in this way I was trying to get some race fitness.

I fell during the Catalan Week and when I returned to Belgium I had a second (correcting) operation on my wrist. In the month of April all the classics came and went without my participation. I did win the kermesse at Bredene on 20th April though, the first of my two wins that season. In the meantime, Marc Demeyer, who had been unconditionally promoted to team-leader by team manager Huysmans (and who was *prepared* by Michiels) was having a brilliant run, coming 2nd in the Tour of Flanders, 4th in Ghent-Wevelgem, 8th in Paris-Roubaix, 4th in the Flèche

Wallonne and 3rd in the Championship of Zurich. He was the saviour of the Flandria team, while I felt as if I had been completely *stabbed in the back* and cast aside. Physically I was having a hard time and depression was looming just around the corner.

After the Sombreffe-Charleroi race on 7th May in which I climbed off, I was not to be seen in the peloton at all during the rest of May and June. Through Dr Verhelst I got to know pharmacologist, Paul Nijs from Zoersel. Since Paul Claeys was beginning to believe Guillaume Michiels' insinuations that I was totally *burned out*, he instructed me to go to America with Nijs to undertake a thorough medical examination. It was America because Paul Nijs had studied at the School of Medicine in Philadelphia and he was convinced about the quality of medical examination which could be carried out there. Paul Claeys was to pay for the plane tickets, our stay and the tests – everything in fact.

On 25th May, we boarded an American Airlines DC-10 at Schiphol in Holland. During the flight I said to Nijs that I thought the engine was making a funny noise. My companion, who had travelled in aeroplanes far less than I had, thought I was joking at first, but when I maintained it he started to fell pretty uneasy. We disembarked at Kennedy Airport in New York while the plane continued on to Chicago. A few seconds after it took off again, an engine caught fire and the DC-10 crashed to the ground. No fewer than 279 people died, making it the worst air disaster in American history.

We hired a car in New York and drove to Philadelphia. At the University of Pennsylvania clinic I undertook all kinds of physical and psychological tests. All of the major organs were examined – my heart, kidneys, adrenal glands, liver, lungs and so on. In the meantime the rumour was going around Belgium (which accountant Sergooris eagerly helped start) that I had been admitted to a mental hospital in America. I can only give one answer to that, if I had been in need of a mental institution at that time, I think I would have saved myself the long journey and made do with a Belgian one.

The tests didn't last the whole day and as I had taken my bike with me, I went on a twenty minute circuit of the huge park in

Philadelphia with Nijs acting as a pacemaker in the car. On one occasion, before I'd realised it, I was riding down the highway until the local police escorted me back on to the right road with its flashing lights on. I was staying in a single room at the hospital, but with a radio, television and telephone and a lounge and bathroom nearby it felt more like an hotel. Nijs was staying at the Holiday Inn and came to watch the tests every day which were carried out by the medical team under Dr Fischer who had once been his own professor.

One evening we were invited to Dr Fischer's home. Cycling wasn't as popular in America as it is now, and therefore he had never seen a professional racing cycle from close up. He would like to have ridden a lap on it, but with those gears it was clear that he wouldn't have been able to manage it. While changing gears he kept forgetting to pedal and it looked really comical.

Other acquaintances of Paul Nijs from his days as a student were two Flemish priests, Father Georges and Father Vince, who ran a mission in the black district of 13th Street; and they were two lovely chaps. During the sermon at the mass we attended the locals were informed that we were two friends from Belgium. This helped us become quickly accepted in the ghetto where normally the presence of whites was not particularly appreciated. Now and then we would go to the priests' homes on an evening to have a game of cards or a glass of beer. Since then, Father Georges has died and Father Vince has returned to Belgium.

On the evening before our return to Belgium, Nijs and I went for a meal in an Italian restaurant on the wide boulevard alongside the Delaware River. While we were tucking into our aperitif one of the Italians suddenly came storming out of the kitchen shouting, *'Signore Maertens! Il campione del mondo!'*

I would never have dreamed that anybody would know who I was in far-away Philadelphia. He immediately treated us to another aperitif. After the starter, main course and dessert, the Italian came to join us for coffee with pousse-café. When we were ready to leave we asked for the bill but they refused to let us pay for anything!

Another coincidental meeting took place on the flight home. Because all DC-10 aeroplanes were grounded for inspection following the accident, we were forced to book onto a Jumbo Jet which, although more comfortable, was also more expensive.

Above the cockpit there was a bar which was being tended by someone from . . . Middelkerke!

"Where do you come from?" he called in a surprised tone when he saw me. He treated us to champagne, although in fact everything was included in the price anyway.

The results of all the tests were positive, and I took Dr Fischer's medical report with me when I went to see Paul Claeys. He was astonished and had to admit that he had been wrong to listen to the false allegations of Guillaume Michiels and his cronies. The cost of the journey, my stay and the examinations came to BF 390,000, and even though Paul Claeys had promised to settle the bill himself, I ended up paying for everything out of my own pocket and I never saw the money again.

In order to remove any doubt, here is the text of Dr Fischer's final verdict:

'To whom it may concern:

Freddy Maertens has been a patient of mine at the Institute of the Pennsylvania Hospital in Philadelphia, Pennsylvania, from May 24 to June 7, 1979. During this time he has had a complete physical and neurologic examination and complete laboratory studies of his urine and blood which reflect the functioning of his kidneys, liver and thyroid gland. Mr Maertens is in excellent physical health and all his laboratory studies have been normal. Dr Nys, his companion, has copies of all these studies which are within normal limits.

In addition, I have seen Mr Maertens and Dr Nys almost daily for psychotherapy sessions to discuss the problems he has had in relationship to drugs. Unbeknownst to him, I've also tested his blood twice weekly and have found no evidence of secretive drug usage.

On the basis of my interviews with Mr Maertens and Dr Nys, I believe that he is not presently addicted to drugs, especially amphetamines and he has an excellent chance to remain off of amphetamines in the future. Though I suspect he will be tempted to use stimulating drugs when he is under competitive pressure, I think he has the inner strength to resist this temptation and

116

in addition the plan that Dr Nys has suggested of having a qualified companion-trainer with Mr Maertens during his competitive season, would prove most helpful.

Please contact me for any additional information or assistance.

Sincerely yours,
[signed]
Newell Fischer, M.D.'

On July 3rd I made my return to the peloton at Kruishoutem. Fate, however, seemed determined to deal me another blow. On the last day of July, in the Scheldt Grand Prix at Schoten, I was getting ready to sprint for second place behind Daniël Willems who had broken clear, when I had a puncture in the final kilometres.

Due to my lack of competitive cycling throughout the season, I was obviously not selected for the world championships in Valkenburg. My second and final victory of the season was achieved on September 5th at Wingene. To celebrate this win Carine and I were invited to the house of my team-mate, Alain De Roo, who was also living in Lombardsijde at the time, where we had a meal of trout. That night as we were lying in bed, our dog suddenly started barking wildly at about twenty to five. I got up to see what was going on. I thought I was dreaming at first, but officials from the Belgian Drug Brigade (BOB) were waiting outside with an order to come and search my house at five o'clock in the morning, which was the earliest time allowed under Belgian law. At around the same time BOB officers were forcing their way into the homes of my parents and my brother Mario. This co-ordinated action came about as a result of an anonymous tip-off, and although I was never able to find out afterwards exactly who it had been, it must have been somebody from the cycling world who was at odds with me and out to get me. Later that morning Alain De Roo wandered casually into the house through the back door, his hands in his shorts pockets.

"All these cars in front of your house, Freddy. Are the BOB here or something?" he nonchalantly asked.

117

He had hardly finished speaking when a BOB officer leaped out of one of the rooms pointing a shotgun at him. They had just about managed to stop short of bringing their carbines for this particular house search. They did make a real meal of it though, wandering backwards and forwards, snooping in the cupboards and going through the contents, making notes, typing things out and so on. They literally wanted to see everything; even what was in the rubbish bin. If I wanted to go to the toilet somebody had to come with me. Our garage was also thoroughly searched, and in the cellar I was made to open the safe. They must have envisaged it being full of Pervitin but they were disappointed. Out of desperation, they took everything out of the medicine cabinet, including my wife's contraceptive pills, and took them away to Professor Heyndrickx's lab.

After this incident Carine and I frequently had to report to the BOB offices in Ostend and the Public Prosecutor's Office in Bruges. Since they had been unable to find anything suspicious, they began to ask us questions about anything and everything including the million francs which Jef Dhondt, my former physio who had followed Pollentier to Splendor, had borrowed from me at a rate of 3% interest. When it came to asking for this money back, he accused me of falsification of documents, claiming that the amount concerned had never been as high as that. The affair came before the small claims court in January 1984 where I was found to be in the right. When Dhondt also lost the case at the Court of Appeal in Ghent, he was ordered to pay the money back to me in monthly instalments, although it still has yet to be completely paid off. Also summoned to the small claims court in Veurne in January 1984 were physio Guillaume Michiels and mechanic Roland Libert. During a house search at Michiels' home just as he was about to set off for the six-day event at Ghent, they did come across amphetamines.

At the end of 1979, due to financial difficulties, Paul Claeys decided to withdraw from cycling sponsorship. There was no longer a team to line up in the Tour of Lombardy, the last of the end of season classics.

When Flandria disbanded it left me out in the cold. Lomme Driessens, who by then was directeur sportif of the Boule d'Or team, promised me that he would find me a place in his team. As an explanation of why nothing ever came of this offer (until a full year later), something else needs to be said here. I was signed to a publicity contract a few years earlier with the biscuit company Vranckaert which brought me BF 150,000 in return for posing for a few photographs. I had been put onto this by Willy Delabastita, the manager of Boule d'Or who was to receive 10% or BF 15,000 for his part.

During the presentation of the Trophée Gan I bumped into the managing director of the cake firm purely by chance and said to him, "Thank you again for the BF 150,000. It was very good money for such a small job."

"Freddy, you're wrong you know," he answered. "It was BF 300,000."

"No it wasn't," I replied. "You've got it wrong. I only received BF 150,000."

"Oh, let's not quibble about it," he said. "I'll send you a copy of the contract."

And there it was in black and white, the amount of BF 300,000 was clearly shown. The difference was that on the place where my signature should have been was Delabastita's. He'd therefore been able to pocket BF 150,000 as well as the BF 15,000 he had received from me and the BF 35,000 commission Vranckaert had given him. In other words, he had made a net total of BF 200,000 for his part in the operation while I got BF 135,000. I therefore instituted proceedings against him.

Driessens was now reassuring me in the restaurant 't Hoeveke in Oostduinkerke, "If you sign this note in which you promise to withdraw legal proceedings against Delabastita, you can ride for Boule d'Or."

I signed and Delabastita was safe, but I still wasn't taken on by the team. I had once again been kicked squarely in the teeth and there was nothing I could do about it but look for a new sponsor while Lomme took on Fons De Wolf and Roger De Vlaeminck.

I rang Lomme and only said the words, "Thanks very much for your *vote of confidence*, Lomme."

20   Labour and Capital

Through Firmin Verhelst I got to know Carlino Menicagli who was to become my new directeur sportif. He in turn brought me into contact with the head of the Italian company, San Giacomo, and a financial agreement was quickly reached. Now that my transfer to Boule d'Or was off I thought the best choice I could make would be to join an Italian team. After everything that had been written about me Belgian sponsors no longer had any faith in me. Like all the other San Giacomo riders I had to undergo a medical examination by the team doctor and this confirmed the results from Philadelphia, that there was nothing wrong with my health.

To prepare for the 1980 season I stayed with Alain De Roo for eighteen days at Montecatini Terme, a spa resort where not only sportsmen but many others with rheumatic complaints went for treatment. Wearing your bathing suit, you descended down steps 60 metres into underground caves and laid on one of the sunbeds where you automatically began to sweat. It wasn't artificial but was simply as a result of the natural sauna conditions. You could feel your pores completely opening up. Once back at the top you were sprayed alternately with hot and cold water. After that you were given another bathing suit and you had to go and rest for half an hour in your room. On certain days there were also mudbaths and massages. Alain and I also did some running and gymnastic exercises on our own initiative. We certainly never had time to become bored at Montecatini Terme.

A few weeks later the company directors offered all the team riders a skiing holiday in Piancavallo. The Italian riders were only allowed to have their wives or girlfriends there for the weekend but Carine and Alain's wife could stay with us for the whole time. Most of the riders in the team were very young, among whom were Visentini, whose talent was then still blossoming, Bortolotto, Martinelli, Corti and Bertacco. While at San Giacomo I got to know an excellent physio, Rino Barone, who still regularly sends me greetings cards. Prior to that he had only worked with football teams, but now he regarded it as a real honour to be able to work with a former cycling world champion.

On January 3rd Alain, our two wives, my daughter Romy and I

took up residence in the communal villa which San Giacomo's manager, Dinardo, had made available to us. During one of the first days there we had BF 120,000 stolen. I had brought this money with me from Belgium because I wanted to open a bank account in Italy and we wouldn't be receiving our first month's wages until March. Carine had put the lights on in the rooms and was looking in her handbag for some money to go shopping when she noticed, to her horror, that all of the money had gone.

We had our suspicions about who had done it. Two of our Italian team-mates lived in a flat just behind our villa and one night all of us had gone to the cinema. The Italians were driving in front of us in their car when suddenly they stopped near a little wood as one of them needed to spend a penny. However, instead of getting back into their car he came running towards us shouting.

"Guess what I've just seen down there," he said.

We followed him and sure enough, in the place he was pointing to was my wallet with our cheques and banker's cards but without the money, of course. We have always thought it was pretty suspicious that he knew exactly where to go for a wee in that wood that night.

After the Six Days at Milan I started in the Grand Prix of Laigueglia. In this, the first race of the season in Italy, I gave up. I still hadn't reached peak fitness and the team management were well aware of this as all they had done was to ask me to turn up at the start. In the Tour of Sardinia, things went better. I completed this stage race and on the stage to Steresa di Callura I even managed to finish second. I didn't take part in Het Volk but entered for the Chronostafetta in Montecatini on March 1st instead. I won the road race, came eleventh in the individual time trial and in the two up time trial I finished third with Bertacco. If someone had told me then that my only victory of the season was already behind me I would have thought they were mad, and yet that's the way it turned out.

Paris-Nice that year was terrible, with storms, rain and sleet making the entire event a nightmare, but I gritted my teeth and finished as second highest Belgian in the final classification.

During the lead up to the sprint in Milan-San Remo I was obstructed by my own team-mate Visentini, otherwise I would have definitely finished in the first three instead of 12th. My 6th places in both the Tour of Campania and the Trophée Pantalica only served to compound in me the belief that I could travel to the Tour of Flanders full of confidence. Compared to the previous season, the only thing missing were my *pilots* to bring me up into a good position for the closing stages. Nowadays it was left to me to find the best position.

In this particular Tour of Flanders Marc Demeyer and I had escaped from the leading group. Due to the circumstances we had no option but to help each other but we didn't say a word the whole time as our parting had signalled the end of our friendship. Yet in the end it was Michel Pollentier, the third member of our trio, who won after successfully attacking Francesco Moser and Jan Raas. These two were watching out for each other the whole time and Michel made the most of it, a skill which he had acquired as early as the junior categories. While the faster men concentrated on each other he would drop back slightly and then suddenly launch himself forward at top speed like a jack-in-the-box. Marc Demeyer eventually finished 5th and I came 6th, so it was just like the good old days at Flandria, except that we were all riding for different teams now.

In Maarkedal, past the Koppenberg climb, I fell because a child was crossing the road when I took a corner. The next night I had an attack of fever as a result of an infection from my injuries and I felt very ill and was pouring with sweat. I remained at home for four weeks, during which time there was no improvement in my condition. By now I was at the end of my tether, so I consulted the Jewish homoeopath Pladys in De Panne, and although I recovered I had lost a great deal of weight. In Italy they didn't believe that there could have been so much wrong with me and I was requested to take another medical examination. Instead of allowing me some rest so that I could return to full strength, the team doctor put me on a course of heavy training which only had the result of making me even more fatigued than I already was. My optimum weight is 70 kgs but at that moment I was substantially less, yet this didn't stop them ordering me to ride in the Giro. The predictable outcome was to take place on the 11th stage between Palinuro and Campotenese, when I arrived outside the time limit. At least that is how it is shown in the record books as with only a few kilometres to go, I still had five minutes to spare. After that, San Giacomo's manager, Dinardo, ordered me to ride every stage ahead of the actual race or otherwise I would not receive my wages.

It was also around that time that I started experiencing difficulties in receiving payments from San Giacomo. I had a contract worth BF 3.5 million, but I never saw anything of the expenses (for such as aeroplane tickets) which they had promised me.

Eventually my monthly wages were no longer paid to me. On June 17th in the Grand Prix of Camaiore, I wore a San Giacomo jersey for the last time. I called in the help of Sporta, the interest organisation run by Maurice Lippens to defend my case, but it didn't do the slightest bit of good. When I was having a difficult time later in my career, Sporta were never of any real use either.

Despite all this I still got on very well with directeur sportif Menicagli, but he was in no position to resist Dinardo and his sharp practices either. It was easy to see how this man had once spent time in jail for being a member of the Mafia. I once played a trick on him while Carine and I were staying at his villa in Empoli. One Sunday he went to a party with his wife and children (including the mischievous little rascal Eddy, named after Merckx).

"You two will have to make do with one glass of wine," Dinardo told us before he set off.

While they were out, in a sense of revenge, we both emptied about thirty bottles of the wine which they had made themselves and kept in their wine cellar and filled them with water. I would love to have seen the look on his face when he discovered it for the first time while entertaining distinguished guests at his table.

I called in a solicitor to guarantee that the rest of my contract would be paid up, but San Giacomo's final offer was that they would pay half of it. It was a case either of accepting their offer or of taking the whole thing to court, so I decided to choose the former option.

The problems with San Giacomo were only one part of the financial mess I was caught up in. To this day I am still owed BF 4.5 million by Flandria. There is a simple explanation for this. I would always say to Paul Claeys, "Just make sure that you sort everything out with Pollentier and Demeyer first, then nobody will have any complaints." When things started to go downhill for the company though, it was me who paid the price, although I still hope to get my hands on part of the money one day.

At the same time I was running into trouble at my local tax office. A certain tax official at Ostend really had it in for me. A balance sheet of my assets was drawn up, a practice usually reserved for large property owners. I ended up having to pay tax on money that I had never received.

Paul Claeys and I were also partners in the Flandria Ranch at Torhout. When the deeds of foundations were drawn up I was to contribute half a million francs which would later be increased to two million. Robert Sergooris was responsible for the accountancy side of it but ended up making off with a great deal of our money. After a memorable boxing bill on which Jean-Pierre Coopman was the main attraction, filling the Flandria Ranch to the rafters, Sergooris disappeared with the takings. He had been carrying out a policy of total mismanagement with the business. The only thing he wanted to do was to make as much money as he possibly could but I just didn't have the time to attend to it all. Willy Verlé, who had been coming to races with me for years, was right when he said that sportsmen shouldn't become involved in business ventures until their active careers are over. I let myself be drawn in, though, while Pollentier always kept his distance from projects like the Flandria Ranch. He was, however, taken in another way. He had invested his money with somebody at a high rate of interest and that was the last he ever saw of it. The moral of the story is: there are always shady characters hanging around those with money.

Together with Marc Demeyer and Paul Claeys, I was a partner in Ninocycle in Ninove, a shop which sold cycles and parts for the wholesale trade. There was a similar shop in Zedelgem but I didn't have a stake in that one. Ninocycle went bust and I had to wave goodbye to my BF 300,000 of starting capital.

Finally, there was the furniture company, Frema, in Jemappes, in which I was also in partnership with Marc Demeyer. This concern, for which Sergooris had taken out an insurance policy, burnt to the ground. The BF 750,000 which I had put in went up in flames with it.

When I was doing well financially, all of the banks were constantly approaching me with investment plans. They knew there was money to be made from me and would treat me to meals in order to discuss them. I hardly ever dared to say no. How many life insurance policies, for example, wouldn't I have endorsed? Yet when I was suddenly in trouble, I was forced to withdraw much of this capital to square my debts. It was during this period that Carine once went to a bank where we had been customers for years to withdraw BF 5,000 but was refused. Ever since that day, nobody has needed to tell my wife what it feels like to be humiliated.

21 Better days may return

After I was fired by San Giacomo my preparations for the following season could begin as early as August 1980. Although I hadn't remained in close contact with Paul Nijs since our trip to Philadelphia, he introduced me to Dirk Merckx, one of his former pupils and holder of an official Belgian coaching certificate. Under his supervision I began to train very hard. Looking back on it perhaps it was too hard (especially all the weight training), since during the first months of the 1981 season I was hardly ever able to get to the front of a race even though I would normally have been *flying* after such a campaign. As well as exercises with weights for the stomach, back and calf muscles and running in the dunes, I also did a great deal of interval training behind a derny. On one freezing cold winter's day my pacemaker, Louis Bouvy, was so frozen that we literally had to lift him from his motorbike.

Paul Nijs was a great believer in the vegetable extracts that he prepared himself and which gave the same stimulating effect as amphetamines. This was completely new to cycling and nobody had tried it before. The programme devised by Dirk Merckx was just as revolutionary, as it was only later that *physical trainers* emerged in the peloton. Lomme Driessens, who managed to find me a place in the Boule d'Or line-up after a year's delay, was really too old to take to these modern theories.

With all due respect to the research and energy which Nijs had put into them, his vegetable drinks were anything but tasty. Maybe some people would be able to take them without any trouble but they always made me want to be sick. I suppose I was being used as a guinea pig in a way. Whenever I was given anything by him before the closing stages of a race I had to tell him what the result was afterwards. In fact the outcome was always the same – I threw up. However, let me repeat that I do not want to detract from all the efforts he put into it.

Having said that, I no longer wish to have anything to do with Dirk Merckx. He used to bring the extracts with him that Nijs had prepared for us. They claim that it was down to them that I returned to the top of the sport at the end of 1980 but I strongly doubt that their methods really had that much effect.

I split with Dirk Merckx at the beginning of the 1981 season. He wanted to become involved with the whole team and that was the last thing he should have tried with Driessens around, but that wasn't the main reason why I parted company with him. I was paying him BF 30,000 a month and was reimbursing his petrol costs. This involved him travelling from Schelle every day and following me on my training runs in his car. After a while of this though, all he would do was suggest a training schedule and stay in my house drinking coffee and the odd glass of Holland gin until I got back. The process would then be repeated in the afternoon. One day I said to Carine, "I'm not giving him 30,000 francs any more just for that." He might as well have simply sent me his schedules. When he discovered I was no longer willing to pay him, he served me with a lawsuit.

Lomme Driessens hadn't changed since our parting in 1977. That's because Lomme never changed at all. He once again told Carine how she ought to make minestrone soup and just like me she conformed to his wishes. Here is an example of what I mean. After the final stage in the Three-Days at De Panne in 1982, Lomme gave Carine the instruction, "Go home and have dinner ready for when we get back and, above all, make sure no-one else is there."

As you might have expected, a couple who lived near Leuven with whom we were friendly, came round to see Carine. She was afraid to let them in though, because she feared Lomme would make an almighty fuss. It had come this far – we were no longer the bosses in our own home.

We didn't really have much choice. Lomme had already been with Boule d'Or for two years when I joined and naturally I was the one who had to do all the adjusting. I was offered a monthly salary of BF 30,000 net and I didn't even have any choice in the matter as I could not point to any outstanding performances in 1980 to strengthen my bargaining position.

Willy Delabastita gave me the choice, "It's take it or leave it," after which, during the same contract negotiations he haughtily added, "anyway, I think 30,000 francs is more than enough for a rider of your quality."

I couldn't really expect many kind words, of course, since our conflict relating to the publicity contract with the biscuit company

Vranckaert in which he had cheated me.

A condition of my being recruited was that I had to undergo a thorough medical examination.

"I don't want to take any risks," said Delabastita in an insinuating tone. Thanks to Lomme, Gust Naessens was my new physio. He was dedicated to his profession and lived at home with his sister. A couple of years ago he died while he was sitting in a tram and somehow it seemed typical that Gust should go in that way. He never wanted to be any trouble to anyone. While I was out training, Gust would stay in the garage remaining in the same posture the whole time, waiting for me to come home so that he could clean me up and massage me.

"Why don't you come in and sit in the living room until Freddy's back," Carine would suggest.

'No *ma'am*, thanks very much,' Gust would always answer.

Carine once found him sleeping under the massage table since he would rather have done that than disturb her in the house.

Whenever Lomme rang from Vilvoorde to say he was coming to Westende, Gust would curse, "Does that mean we're going to be stuck with him for the whole afternoon? For God's sake why doesn't he let us get on with our work!"

Gust lived in with us for a while but when we first suggested the idea to him, he didn't want to know.

"Why don't you just look for a little flat for me somewhere around here," he said. "A room with a bed will do."

After the first night he spent there (or at least we thought he had), he arrived at our home in the morning absolutely shattered. It seems he hadn't been able to find the flat that we had pointed out to him. Despite the fact that he had a key to our house, he hadn't dared to come in and had slept in his car.

That evening Carine went with him to make sure he would definitely find were he was supposed to be going. The next morning however, Gust looked worn out again.

"What happened?" we asked.

"I haven't slept a wink all night," he answered. "I ran my sheets under the tap because they were covered in gnats and then I wrapped myself in the wet sheets."

After much persuasion on our part, he finally agreed to stay in our guest room. Every morning though, after our meal, he would go upstairs straightaway, no matter what time it was.

"Why don't you stay downstairs for a while?" Carine would then say. "Don't you like watching the news on television?"

"No *ma'am*, thanks very much."

When I became world champion for the second time in Prague, Carine and her friend Christa went up to Gust and they both gave him three kisses.

"Thank you for everything you've done," said Carine. "You've played a big part in this world title."

Gust was very proud and beaming, yet he still kept himself in the background again. If Carine and Christa hadn't dragged him over with them to come and have a glass of champagne and something to eat with us, he would have disappeared off on his own again.

Good old Gust. What a smashing man.

Lomme later told all and sundry that he had stopped me touching a single drop of alcohol during the winter of 1980-81 which led up to the season of my resurrection, but that was in fact a lie. If you were in his company he didn't mind you having a glass of champagne or wine. However if he (or Willy Verlé for that matter) found out that I had been drinking behind his back, there was hell to pay, as happened when Lomme discovered I had been to the casino in Middelkerke with Raoul Bouve. Yet when the whole team – Driessens and Delabastita included – were spotted by Raoul Bouve and director Luc Rammant in the same casino with the drink flowing freely as they had their meal, the story went no further.

That winter Michel Pollentier and I met each other by chance at a chat show for sporting personalities. The outcome of it was a meal with our wives, and since then Michel and I – as far as group training with our own teams will allow it – are again regularly out on the road together. If there ever was a period in which we kept our distance as a result of the distorted statements which had appeared in the newspapers, it never went as far as making us resentful of each other.

Michel was about to embark on his own nightmare season. Although he was team leader of Vermeer-Thijs, he managed only one win and that was at the kermesse race at Sleidinge. His sub-standard performances must be put down to private reasons. An inspector at the bank with whom he had entrusted his money at a rate of interest higher than normal, fled the country with

Michel's money. It came as a crushing blow to his morale. Upon his recovery following psychological treatment and convalescence, he told gathered journalists, "It is only now that I can understand all the things that Freddy Maertens has been through. His misery has been the same as mine."

When things started to go better for me he was able to use me as an example of what he could still achieve. I even tried to get Boule d'Or to sign him for the 1982 season so that there would be a reunion between us. Our bosses preferred Daniël Willems however and Michel found a place with Safir.

Marc Demeyer also had a hard time of it in 1981. After impressive performances with the Capri-Sonne team during the closing stages of the Tour of Flanders and Ghent-Wevelgem, fate was to take a hand just before the Tour de France. He struggled on despite an injury to his achilles tendon but was finally forced to have his leg put into plaster and take a complete rest for eight weeks. Partly due to his business problems, he had to endure several difficult months. His planned comeback which was due to take place with the Splendor team in 1982 was never to happen as, shortly before the team presentation, he died suddenly. The peloton had lost its locomotive forever.

22   Prelude in a Minor Key

I have already said that the only reason things did not go as well as I had expected during the first part of the 1981 season was probably the over-intensity of my training schedule with Dirk Merckx. Nevertheless it began well in the Ruta del Sol. In the second stage my team-mate Havik won by a mile after another Boule d'Or rider, Frits Pirard, had left a gap and I won the sprint for second place. Two days later I was awarded victory in the stage to San Javier after Noël Dejonckheere was adjudged to have been given a push by his team-mate, Geert Malfait, and was subsequently disqualified. Everybody thought I would win regularly during the early part of the season but, as a result of the factors mentioned above, it was not to be. That's still the only thing I can put it down to.

On the last day of the Ruta del Sol I fell as a result of another illegal manoeuvre by Dejonckheere. I was left with a swollen hand and my back also began to give me pain again. Despite this I apppeared for the start of Het Volk. One of my faults has always been that I have never complained enough. Many riders made a drama out of nothing, but that was not my style. If something wasn't too serious I didn't think it was worth the trouble to make a fuss and use it as an excuse. Maybe I should have done so more often.

I retired during Het Volk and because my hand remained swollen I consulted Dr Verhelst. An X-ray revealed that when I fell in the Ruta del Sol I had broken two fingers. Lomme still didn't believe it, doubting the expertise of the doctor.

Anyway, with a *hexilite* bandage which automatically adjusted to the shape of the hand and wrist I felt slightly better. It was only the results which failed to improve. I did manage 10th in the Circuit of the Flemish Ardennes finishing at Ichtegem but in yet another sub-arctic Paris-Nice I retired in the fourth stage. In Milan-San Remo, the Flèche Wallonne and in the Tour of Flanders I fell. It was certainly my year when it came to falling even though my critics had already been saying I was downright dangerous on the road. All the falls I had that year, however, can only be put down to fate. Often it wasn't through any fault of my own. If everybody had been able to steer as skilfully as I could in those days, I wouldn't have had such a problem with it.

My fall in the Tour of Flanders left me with a swollen foot and that was far from the ideal way to start Ghent-Wevelgem. I had a go anyway, in spite of it, although I had to drop out in my home village of Lombardsijde and ended up riding home. Carine had been watching the race from a bit further up the road and when she saw the riders pass she could see that I wasn't among them. When she arrived home she found me sitting on the doorstep as I didn't have a key with me. The series of crashes continued in Paris-Roubaix and the Henninger Turm. It may sound difficult to believe but all of this was nothing to do with a lack of concentration. It just seemed as though unknown forces were at play.

The night before the Four Days of Dunkirk, I was ordered to report with my team-mates to a hotel, but really I had no appetite for this stage race which I had already won four times. I telephoned assistant manager Willy Jossart to say that I hadn't been able to find the hotel. The following morning I rang him to announce that I would report at the start after all. Jossart's reply was that I needn't bother as Werner Devos had already been called up to replace me.

Shortly before that, Driessens had suffered a slight heart attack and therefore, in theory, should have started to act more calmly. Try getting Lomme to do something like that, though. Perhaps he had suffered the heart attack because I had done nothing at all during the the entire first half of the season. In any event, he seriously began to wonder whether it had been worthwhile bothering with me. There was also a certain amount of ill-feeling among the other riders in the team as so often happens when the leader is not performing well.

Following the Championship of Zurich I appeared only in kermesse races in May. It was the only alternative and what was worse was that I didn't even find it frustrating. As the results continued to remain sub-standard, I became increasingly apathetic and didn't put as much into it as I should have done. I admit, therefore, that I wasn't free of blame myself. An example of my apathy was when I had already given up by the second part of the first stage in the Tour de l'Oise on May 17th. This explains a lot, if not everything. Psychologically I was at a low ebb, partly because all those months of preparation with Dirk Merckx had failed to produce the results I was hoping for and partly because I couldn't get my tax problems out of my mind. I never felt tempted to pack it all in though, and no matter how badly it was going I stuck at my training. Sometimes I would retire from a race and then ride home on my bike.

Willy Verlé, who had been taking me to races during those difficult weeks, told me after the Coastal Arrow Race at Knokke-Heist on May 21st that he felt no longer able to continue. He had been watching my performance in the Coastal Arrow and although I had impressed during the race, I suddenly retired without having shown any signs of needing to do so. His words that evening gave me food for thought, as he had been one of the few who had remained loyal to me at that time. He always took me to meetings in his BMW and I was even carpeted by Delabastita for accepting his help.

"Who is your sponsor, anyway?" he asked, "Boule d'Or or Autohandel Verlé."

Verlé was often a thorn in Lomme's side as well and he stayed with me until July 1983 when one day he suddenly let me go. This is what happened. Because I feared the tax people would confiscate my car, I wanted to sell it. After the criterium at Londerzeel, Verlé said to me, "I think I've found a buyer for your car: Eric Vanderaerden. You just have to bring it to my garage so that Eric can come and have a look at it."

That's exactly what I did and Verlé sold my car to Vanderaerden and from that day on took him to races. Vanderaerden's team-manager, Peter Post, would not tolerate Verlé getting involved in the team's internal affairs though and showed him the door. Since then, Verlé has never attended another cycle race.

The first race following Verlé's threat that he would leave me to my own devices, in May 1981, took place in Wielsbeke where I actually managed to finish 3rd. It wasn't only Verlé's harsh words that were responsible for the sudden turnaround, an even greater incentive was provided by the Burgomaster of Wielsbeke, Noël Demeulenaere, who gave me so much help (and still does) in my search for a solution to my financial problems.

Before the start he urged me, "I'm going to ride in the race car for a few laps and woe betide if you abandon here!"

It was the only way I could have returned all the favours he had done for me, so while I was on his home territory I felt morally obliged to do my very best. Robert *Blondie* Deramoudt, who had accompanied me to the race, opened the boot of his car on every lap, convinced that in the atrocious weather conditions it wouldn't be long before I would call it a day. In the previous few months he had hardly seen any other outcome. To his absolute amazement however, I defied wind and rain and on every lap he had to close his car boot again. He just couldn't work out what was happening.

That 3rd place in Wielsbeke was the lift I had been waiting for for such a long time. Steadily I began to live totally for my profession again, without it appearing to anyone watching to be producing positive results. In the Midi Libre, which was ridden in almost tropical heat and which had never been one of my favourite races even in my best years, I gave up the battle during the second stage. As had happened in the Giro the year before I rode ahead of the race for the remaining stages and at night continued to stay in the same hotel as the rest of my team-mates. In the Tour de l'Aude, which is less demanding than the Midi Libre, I did reach the finish. More than that though, before the actual stage began I would complete a training ride every day. Later, when my comeback in the Tour de France was a fact, people often talked about Maertens' *secret weapon*. Well, there was nothing secret about that weapon, it had been built while putting all the countless kilometres under my wheels during the Tour de l'Aude and it certainly didn't misfire.

Dr Derluyn from Izegem had, in the meantime, become my sports doctor. Annie Monseré put me in touch with him as he had been both their neighbour and Jean-Pierre's physician. Because there were so many rumours circulating about me, I didn't want to hurry things too much. After a thorough medical examination he came to the conclusion that the experiments which Paul Nijs had carried out on me did not suit my system. As a result of this, Dr Derluyn began to treat me with specific aims. He made sure that the natural elements in my body that were used up the most and the quickest were replenished on time with preparations. In the Belgian Championship on June 21st in Putte, I didn't feel quite strong enough to jump up to Roger De Vlaeminck who had escaped. I was obviously still short of the required strength but that day gave me more self-confidence. In the Tour de France it was my self-confidence which was to shine through.

23 Unravelling the Mystery

Despite the continuous progress I was making, it looked for a long time as though I wouldn't be selected for the Tour de France. I have to thank Lomme's wife, Maria, for my last-minute selection. I was in a state of panic being afraid I would be left at home so, in desperation, I rang her up to ask if she would put in a good word with Lomme for me. Since the first period in which I worked with Lomme, I had always been the apple of Maria's eye. She is a real motherly type and she liked Carine as well. Lomme would later get very annoyed when I was telling journalists that it was down to Maria that I had taken part in the Tour, but that was the truth, pure and simple. It was as well she convinced Lomme as I certainly couldn't have counted on any good turns from Delabastita, in view of our personal emnity.

Gery Verlinden was selected as team-leader for the overall classification and I was not given any privileged status, but I was just very happy to have been given the chance to start in the prologue in Nice on June 25th. While I was warming up for this short time trial I crashed into a woman who had clambered over a safety barrier and was crossing the street. This resulted in me arriving late at the starting ramp, and when I set off the stopwatch was already running and I finished a lowly 66th. The press had a good snigger as they dismissed my explanation of what had happened as a feeble excuse.

"If it hadn't have been for that I would have definitely finished near the top," I assured them.

They nodded sympathetically but obviously didn't believe me.

When I won the stage the following day, starting and finishing in Nice, they had no choice but to believe me. Although it was only run over 97kms it was a tough stage as many climbs had been included in the circuit. From the very beginning some hard riding took place. The continuous drizzle also made the roads very slippery so that, on the descents in particular, you had to take risks. A couple of days before that we had familiarised ourselves with the route and I had great misgivings about how it would turn out, but now it was going perfectly. I was still feeling very fresh as we entered the final 15kms, which were totally flat, and I realised I had a chance in the sprint. My expectations were fulfilled when, in the last straight, I came through beautifully from Kelly's wheel and nobody could get past me. I gave out a huge cheer. At long last! I was completely overcome but I didn't quite start to cry. In the tour caravan there was a mixture of consternation and mistrust – how was this possible?

"I have always said that I would bring Freddy back!" declared Lomme triumphantly as he was hanging around my neck for the first time in ages.

That was the only thing that mattered that day and all interest in the team time trial went out of the window. I managed to get hold of Carine on the telephone and she sounded even happier than me. There was only one topic of conversation among the journalists that evening – what was going to happen next with Maertens? The general view was, 'Don't worry, the day after tomorrow he'll be ridden into the ground.'

They were seriously mistaken there, though. Two days after Nice I won on the wide boulevard at Narbonne Plage. I knew the finish like the back of my hand as earlier in the year there had been a stage finishing there in the Midi Libre. On that day, as I had already retired, I sat on a terrace bar studying events closely as the riders stormed up to the finishing line. This meant I knew exactly what to do this time! I waited until the ideal moment and shot past Freuler. My second stage victory was in the bag and the feeling of disbelief in the tour caravan gathered momentum.

In the preparation leading up to the sprint I was given a great deal of support by Gery Verlinden and by Ronald De Witte especially, while Alain De Roo also did some great work to keep the peloton together. Lomme was now in seventh heaven and made sure he was with me posing before the photographers, even though he had hardly given me a second glance the whole season. Flowers may wither and champions may come and go but one thing is sure: Lomme will always have all the time in the world for the man of the moment.

The Pyrenees were not going to stop me, and by the time we rode into my own country on the stage from Roubaix to Brussels on July 8th, nobody could take the green jersey away from me any more. The Belgians were now cheering for me, something that hadn't happened for a long time. I wasn't filled with bitterness at the fact that thousands of people were suddenly behind me now that things were going well for me, though I had previously been a target for their abuse. It simply filled me with satisfaction. I needed to summon up a bit of humbleness about the way they had let me fall. Someone who had been retiring from nearly every race like I had could not have expected any sympathy.

In Brussels I once again beat Freuler. On the afternoon, on the second part of the stage to Zolder, I sold the victory to Eddy Planckaert. Lomme had no knowledge of this but Planckaert's team-manager, Berten De Kimpe, did. The following day I kept victory in the stage from Beringen to Hasselt for myself, yet in return for the favour of the previous day I was almost *stabbed in the back* by Eddy Planckaert and his brother Walter. There's nothing much you could teach the Planckaerts about sly tricks.

I got over the Alps with a pair of team-mates by my side. One of them was Ronald De Witte who was certainly a better climber than me but who also realised that it was financially beneficial for the whole team if I were to reach Paris in the green jersey unscathed. For that reason, he accompanied me in the stragglers' *bus*. Every time we reached the foot of a col he would try to follow the tempo of the climbers, but could never manage it and we would always catch him up. He would then drop to the back of the *bus* where he even found it difficult to keep up with us. Every evening we tried to convince him that he would be better off just staying with us, but by the following day he would have forgotten again and would be off trying to stay with the leaders no matter what it cost.

I set the seal on my performances in the whole of the tour by winning my fifth stage on the Champs Elysées in Paris. I had now won the green jersey for the third time in my career.

The inevitable question everyone was asking throughout the tour was: 'What was the explanation for this miraculous comeback? What was the real background to this amazing resurrection? There was all sorts of speculation, with new and ever more sensational reasons being given constantly.

Let me answer this once and for all: there was absolutely no mystery attached to my return to the top in the 1981 Tour. If that had been the case and I had been keeping it quiet since then, I would have made it known in this book. I'm afraid, however, there is no secret to be revealed. I hope that people believe this and don't think that I intend to carry it to my grave. What good would it do me to remain silent now? If I say nothing it is simply because there is nothing to say. I surely can't be expected to serve up a marvellous and exciting but totally ficticious intrigue just to satisfy people's thirst for sensation, can I?

The key to my return to form in that Tour de France was based on two factors. First of all, I had quietly been bringing myself back to full fitness for a month in order to reach my peak in the Tour. This was something that the outside world knew nothing about and is precisely why the effects were so surprising and unbelievable. People living near me would no doubt also have been scratching their heads in disbelief during that period. They would have seen me, covered in sweat, riding behind the derny in the afternoon and the next day they would have read in the newspaper that the day before I had retired from a race for the umpteenth time. However, I was just *gearing myself up* in my own way. Secondly, during this Tour I was well away from my financial worries for the first time. I didn't have to answer the telephone, and when I rang Carine she would never say anything about any new problems which were threatening us. I was relaxed, as a professional rider should be. He should only have to think about one thing and that is racing. These two factors – the physical desire to reach my old level, together with the removal of all unnecessary ballast – are the only explanation I can give for the way I suddenly found such form.

Beyond that there is no question of any mystery; in other words it is not true that I had discovered a wonder pill. I only allowed myself to be judiciously treated by Dr Derluyn, and I was excellently looked after by Gust Naessens. With the all-seeing eye of Dr Derluyn, I wouldn't have needed to venture outside his knowledge to experiment, for that matter. The irrefutable evidence that I hadn't done anything illicit in this Tour can be shown by all the dope controls I had to go through in those weeks. My opponents might then add that cortisone produced in your own body can't be traced at these dope controls. My answer to that would be – *so what!* Cortisone has got nothing to do with it. Dr Derluyn only made sure that the important shortages in my body were replenished very quickly. I didn't have any *bombs* in my body then, something journalists would have had you believe because they could find no other easy explanation for my comeback.

Insinuations about me appeared in several papers; some were nastier than others. The Dutchman, Joop Holthausen, proved to be the uncrowned champion of this sport with his article in *Het Parool* on Monday 6th July. The following is taken from the article:

'The question marks remain. Is it Driessens, who has an enormous influence on some of the riders, who has used the mysteries of Catholicism to get Freddy going? That morning he went to the holy mass at Nantes with Maertens. Does his strength come out of the censer or from a totally different, more suspicious container?'

His behaviour is extremely strange. Not only his manner during TV interviews, not even his few-word answers, but also his attitude in the peloton. "He is barmy. He's riding with two cogs heavier (a much larger gear, ed.) than the rest of us." A big gear? Hasn't the tour doctor, Philippe Miserez, said that that is precisely what should no longer be possible? That it was the use of the big gear which was supposedly responsible for Maertens downfall in the first place? Yet he is still using it. He drifts through the peloton but no longer falls over pebbles like he did at the start of the season.'

"Knocked off my balance" was the excuse back then. Yet they keep their eyes peeled if Maertens is riding at the front. "Look out, there goes Freddy!" Tongue hanging out and squeezing through. And then after the race the tongue again and his hands flat with his little fingers on the outside. "He looks like a spastic," says one of his team-mates. One of his colleagues: "We don't begrudge him it, but this is bad for cycling. Maertens is floating. People can see that as well." Is it naturally or chemically induced, this return to the top by Maertens? If it's natural it points to Driessens. Fons De Wolf, who was leader of Driessens' team last year: "Lomme knows how to deal with certain types of people. Remember, he has been with him since October and love can work at once. I don't think that it is Driessens" influence. He can't do anything. But we'll just have to wait and see. We'll see how it goes with Freddy." The peloton is split between admiration and pity, some riders take the mickey out of him by riding to the front the way he does with their tongues hanging out."

It's as though I was riding round at the time like a mindless madman. During the 1981 Tour, I only fell a couple of times. On the stage from Rochefort-sur-Mer to Nantes, for example, it was

Marcel Tinazzi's fault. We had to take a turn to the right and he rode straight ahead. What could I do? Falling is only human, especially when it is caused by something completely out of your own control.

Sometimes, when another slur appeared in a newspaper, I would go and have a word with the journalist responsible on the morning of a stage.

"You've shown you can do a lot on a racing bike, haven't you," I would say to them.

The sort of explanation that someone like that would offer was that he hadn't come up with the story himself but somebody had told him it. Now and then I would go and demand an explanation from a rider for the comments they had been quoted as saying. Once I went to see Gerrie Knetemann after he had made denigrating comments about me in an interview with *Humo* magazine. Sometimes, after somebody had said they found the way I was acting in the peloton suspicious, I would deliberately ride behind them for a while and eventually ask them, "Do you call the way you're riding now, riding in a straight line?"

I'm afraid riders can act so childishly when they get together. They can be just like nursery school children. On one of the stages in the Giro an Italian was riding at the front of the peloton and noticed a hole in the road some distance ahead.

"Attenzione: buco!" he shouted.

Yet who was it who ended up in the *buco?* The Italian of course. From that day on, he's had the nickname *Buco.*

A few days after the final stage in the Tour on the Champs Elysées, I was welcomed back like the prodigal son in the criterium at Aalst. I hoped to be able to pay off some of my tax debts with the starting money I would receive from these criteriums. The tax people were still after me and the threatening letters and telephone calls didn't stop, my financial plight became ever more serious. My original monthly salary had in the meantime been increased to BF 30,000 with an additional clause that it would be revised again if I were to win the world championship in Prague.

After the criteriums, I took part in the Tour of Germany. Officially I didn't win a stage in this event, but I did sell one to Didi Thurau. I retired in my last four races before Prague (at Zottegem, Zingem, Sint-Pieters-Leeuw and the 'Grape Race' at

Overijse). I amply compensated for this though, by riding twice as many kilometres behind a moped. That interval training was a lot more useful to me than riding kermesses, especially as by doing that I was able to prepare myself in a *natural* way.

On the Monday before Prague Carine was emptying our postbox when she noticed that among the post there was an envelope from the tax office and quickly slipped it out of the way.

"What has the postman brought today?" I asked.

"Here, have a look," she replied and handed the whole pile except for that particular, letter thinking that if it was another threatening letter like some of the ones we had already had, it would be an enormous strain on my concentration.

That Wednesday, a few days after the Grape Race at Overijse, my brother-in-law Lionel and I went to see the race Maffle-Mouscron-Maffle. On the way there, something happened which almost wrote off my world championship hopes after all the intense preparation I had been putting in. We were passing a *station wagon* in Zarren in West Flanders and because it was very foggy I said to Lionel who was driving my BMW, 'Follow that wagon so that you've got something to focus on.' However by the side of the road was a lorry with one of its wheels off. The driver of the wagon in front of us was unable to avoid it in time and we ploughed into the *station wagon*. We were thrown to our left just as another lorry was coming in the opposite direction and it pushed our BMW sideways for quite a way. Apart from the slight groin injury my brother-in-law suffered, we were both miraculously unhurt. In a nearby house, the people were very helpful to us and when we set off, I left them one of my jerseys as a souvenir. Once we had made a statement to the police we were allowed to go home. Because I had missed the race, I did a 250 kilometre training session behind a derny in the afternoon, still shaking from the shock.

The next day I departed for Prague.

24   The Desperado in Town

One of the features of every world championship I took part in during my career was the tension in the Belgian team, but in the meeting of the team-managers and BWB members in Prague, it ended up as a direct hand-to-hand confrontation between Lomme Driessens and Fred De Bruyne. What gave rise to it was an interview in *Sport* magazine in which Lomme had accused the other teams of massive incompetence. At stake was a place behind the wheel of the team car.

After this meeting Lomme came looking for me and said, "Come on, we're going home, we've nothing to stay here for. If they won't let me drive the team car you've got no chance of becoming world champion."

"Hang on a minute, Lomme!" I replied. "I've put so much into my training that I'm not going to go straight home."

Eventually Florent Van Vaerenbergh successfully acted as mediator. Lomme climbed down and reconciled himself to sitting alongside Fred in the team Skoda. I somehow doubt, however, that there was much friendly conversation between the two of them during the race.

The gathering of the Belgian team was to follow the same pattern as in previous years: whoever thought they had a chance of winning had to say so. As usual nearly everyone put their hands up. I only had Gery Verlinden there with me as a helper. Herman Van Springel offered to help Roger De Vlaeminck and Claude Criquielion told us he would be riding in the service of Fons De Wolf.

There was scarcely any appropriate food for a cyclist available in Czechoslovakia. Before we departed, however, Gust Naessens had been far-sighted enough to make a list of the ingredients that Carine should bring with her when she came with her friend Christa and Willy Verlé and his wife. This was to suit Gery Verlinden and me ideally during the race. Physio's who hadn't planned this in advance were forced to improvise. They were able to get hold of sugar and tea but not of such food as rice tarts. Gust, therefore, had done a great job and we made sure we hadn't told anyone else.

On the evening before the world championship, BWB doctor

Daniëls was to come and apply a *drip* which I had been given by Dr Derluyn. The use of these drips is not uncommon in cycling. The infusion consists of liquid food which enters the bloodstream directly, the purpose of which is to greatly diminish the chances of diarrhoea during a race. Because the contents needed to be given before the evening meal, I lay on my bed waiting for the arrival of Dr Daniëls. In spite of his promise, he never turned up. He had stayed behind at the reception which was taking place after the amateur race in which the Belgian Rudy Rogiers had finished 2nd. In the end Gery Verlinden had to give me the drip.

When I eventually went downstairs at around ten o'clock to eat, the kitchen was already shut. Willy Verlé's wife suggested to the staff that she would prepare the evening meal herself. We tried to tip them generously but it did no good. All I was given were two ham sandwiches, two slices of tomato and three slices of cheese. I had to make do with that. Downstairs, several Belgian sponsors were sitting having a drink and of course they were having a fine time watching this scene unfold: 'What's Maertens doing down here at half past ten if he is hoping to become world champion tomorrow?'

At five o'clock the next morning Gust brought Verlinden and me our cream cheese with honey and two egg-yolks to our room, something which is very easily digestible. It was still too early to go downstairs and eat in the restaurant so we decided to take a little nap. We overslept, however, and almost missed the bus which was to take us to the start.

I shot downstairs in my track suit and found Carine and Christa who had both been anxiously wondering why I was taking so long. All the other riders had already set off, and on the table there were only the empty plates and cups and some bread and meat that they had left behind. I was in a hurry to clear some space for myself and I reacted to my nervous state by making a wild gesture which sent a couple of eggs flying off the table. It was just at the precise moment they were hurtling away before splattering on to the ground that a colossus of a woman appeared out of the kitchen. She really laid into me. In the Eastern bloc, playing with your food was something you should never do. In the evening after the world championship race was over, the female giant clearly had not forgotten this incident, since when we were all sitting at the table waiting to be served, she left me until the very last.

144

In contrast to Ostuni, where I had the support of several Belgian riders, I had to do it in Prague helped by only one, Gery Verlinden. When a small group escaped in which my only team-mate was Herman Van Springel who didn't stand a chance of winning as he did not have the legs for the final sprint, the other Belgian riders let him get away and the gap gradually increased. I said to Verlinden, "Listen, you'll have to get riding. If we can close the gap I'll be happy with you and you can drop out." From then on, Gery put in a great amount of work, successfully, and that is something for which I will always be grateful to him.

After the definitive leading group had been formed, in which the Italians had the most representation, *Wolfijzer* (that was Fons De Wolf's nickname) asked me, "What shall we do? We're not going to get in each other's way are we?"

'No, of course not,' I replied. 'If you can get away I'll stop.'

It was obvious to me, though, that with so many Italians around he wouldn't be able to succeed. Two circuits before the end I checked with the Italian, Masciarelli, what the lie of the land was.

'If Moser can get away with riders who aren't as fast as him, he becomes our top man,' I was informed. 'As long as this group stays together we are all riding for Saronni, and that includes Moser.'

It was then that I knew that I had to take Saronni's wheel.

In the last but one circuit I had an awkward moment according to those who were watching me, but it was in fact only pretence. I was playing a little game. The other Belgians who were still in the leading group were coming up to me offering their services to me for the final sprint, hoping to earn a bit of cash. Firstly though, they had ridden just as many kilometres as I had and would therefore be at least as tired as me and secondly, I had come to a similar arrangement in my amateur days with Ludo Van Der Linden and it had turned out to be costly to me.

That is why I replied to the Belgians' offer, 'Thanks but there's no need. I'm shattered.'

I played a game of all or nothing and clung on to the back of the group. This made Lomme furious, and he gave Fred the order to drive up alongside me so that he could lay into me, 'The sprint's coming up and all you're doing is lazing about at the back! For God's sake get to the front!'

Earlier on he had also given Willy Verlé a mouthful because

he had allegedly given me my drinking bottle with champagne one circuit too early. However, Lomme had forgotten that I never drank all the champagne in one go but had it in small sips at intervals.

I didn't let Driessens' animated words bother me because I knew that I couldn't let it be seen too early that I was planning to sit on Saronni's wheel. While I was still right at the back as we came to the start of the final climb, Battaglin shot out of the group. I had to keep myself cool as it was still too early to respond.

I kept impressing on myself, 'Only right at the top, just before the bend to the left towards the finish line I'm going to get on Saronni's wheel.'

I pushed the pedals easily to get forward, shoving with my elbows here and there to get past the others, and after a bit of duelling with Hinault (who wasn't born yesterday either), I'd done what I set out to do: to get on Saronni's wheel. Baronchelli was at the front and tried to make a move at the left-hand bend. If I had gone to the right of Saronni at that moment, I wouldn't have been able to do anything else but follow Baronchelli. I had seen it clearly though, and stayed behind *Saronni* which gave me the advantage of being able to pass him both on the left and the right. Everything was clear in my mind that day and I worked it all out to the finest detail. While I was taking Saronni's wheel, I kept an eye on the opposition by looking under my arm and could see that Hinault had taken my wheel.

I started to sprint at the exact moment that I was sure that Hinault wouldn't be able to get past me. That is how, using my 52x13 gear, I became world champion for the second time. I hadn't dared to use my twelve as the final straight went slightly uphill with the wind against us, and because we had already ridden 281 kilometres of the fairly taxing course.

Carine, Christa and Raoul Bouve were standing beyond the bend after the finishing line. In the euphoric state which had overtaken me, I free-wheeled over to them.

"Are you absolutely sure you won, Freddy?" Carine questioned me. She had heard the Czech commentator continually mentioning the name of the fast finishing Hinault and without being able to understand what he was actually saying had thought he must have won.

I hugged her, cheering, "Of course I'm sure."

From an article in one of the newspapers, it would appear that one Dutch journalist decided that he had first seen me in the arms of a *platinum blond bimbo*. That must have been Christa then; we certainly had a good laugh about that afterwards.

As was expected of the champion, I appeared before the radio and television journalists, one of whom was Théo Mathy of RTBF television to whom I told my story. Sitting alongside him was Eddy Merckx who had been his co-commentator throughout the race. Although praising my performance and saying that I had ridden a good tactical race, he immediately added that the circuit hadn't been a very difficult one in spite of the fact that only the week before he had stated that it was not an ideal finish for sprinters. While at the microphone, Mathy looked back with us to my first world title in Ostuni where, according to the commentator, Merckx had played a significant role. As I had no intention of being a spoilsport, I agreed with what they were saying. Many people think that that was the moment Merckx and I came closer together but, in reality, our relationship has remained pretty much as it always was.

Driessens ordered me not to go to the press conference as several articles had appeared in the days leading up to the world championship which were not to his liking. Now was his chance to take revenge in his own way; yet it was me who had to suffer for it later.

I went back from the dope control in the car with Lomme and Fred. The two directeurs sportifs who had been going at it like hammer and tongs before the race were now the best of friends.

"Wasn't it a great performance by *our* rider, Lomme?" said Fred.

"Yes, but we worked well together didn't we Fred?" added Lomme.

And so the two of them carried on like blood brothers as though everything had been sweetness and light between them.

Suddenly Fred asked, "Lomme, now you must tell me how Freddy prepared to become world champion."

"I'll explain it to you," replied Lomme. "I made him train day and night and I mean that literally. It wasn't unusual for me to send him off on a ride with lamps on his bike."

"Is that really true?' replied an astounded Fred. I played along with Lomme's comical speech and in deadly seriousness I said, "Yes. Sometimes Lomme made me go out and start training at half past three in the morning."

Fred told that story later to anyone within earshot. So listen all you riders. If you want to win the world championship you have to fix lights on to your bike.

When we arrived at our hotel I was still in my racing kit. A number of pressmen were waiting for us in the foyer and I answered their questions until national team doctor Daniëls suddenly walked in clutching a cigar and came up to me and offered me his hand.

"I'm not shaking hands with you," I blurted out. "The only thing you're good for is going to receptions and not keeping appointments. Where were you yesterday when you were supposed to be giving me a *drip?*

"Don't be mad Freddy, I only wanted to offer my congratulations," he tried to calm me.

"I don't need your good wishes," I replied.

He would avenge my attack the following year during our stay for the world championship at Goodwood by accusing me of having taken a *drip* with cortisone.

I have often been asked which of my two world titles gave me the greater pleasure. My answer to that is as follows; in Ostuni it was imperative that I didn't lose or otherwise the journalists would have written me off. They would have come to the conclusion, "He can't do it when the chips are down." In contrast to that, Prague was for me the day on which I showed that my successes in the Tour de France could not be put down to good fortune. Since the Tour doubts were being expressed again as I was once again not finishing in many races. What people didn't realise, though, was the fact that I had been training like a man possessed. Because of that, it is the victory in the sprint in Prague which I will always treasure the most. I have watched the video of it on numerous occasions and it still gives me a warm glow when I see it.

As a compensation for the unavoidable stress which had built up going to Prague, I let off some steam. After I had won the criterium in Sint-Niklaas, I was tucked away with Gust Naessens in our hotel as the Grand Prix Eddy Merckx was coming up. I wasn't particularly interested in this time trial, not least because I felt that Driessens had not demanded anything like enough starting money. I therefore decided to stick half of my right hand in plaster and show it to Lomme saying that I had fallen during a training ride. Lomme fell for it and telephoned to withdraw my entry.

I never received all the bonus that Boule d'Or promised me for winning in Prague nor the Fiat Panda and the Bauknecht kitchen I was supposed to get. At the last minute, I was called up to ride in Paris-Brussels where I ended up retiring from the race. I was upset that Boule d'Or had signed Daniël Willems for the 1982 season as I thought it was a totally unnecessary move. After all, wasn't I the world champion? Lomme, however, thought we would make an ideal combination and wanted to make us into the perfect pairing. What Driessens couldn't have known at the time was that assistant directeur sportif Willy Jossart, who had once been Willems' manager, was to use the new man as an instrument not only to get rid of me, but to get rid of Lomme as well.

25　The Drunkard

Apart from Daniël Willems, the young Marc Sergeant was also drafted in to strengthen the Boule d'Or team and I was expected to teach Sergeant the tricks of the trade. He came on holiday with Gust Naessens, Carine, Romy and me to Madesimo in the winter of 1981-82. My thoughts about Marc Sergeant are that he's a really nice lad who to this day has just lacked that little something to become one of the really top riders.

Anyway, I got on with him a thousand times better than I did with Willems. From the beginning I was against the arrival of Willems but Delabastita and Jossart never asked my opinion on the matter. I had a feeling even then that Boule d'Or signing Willems was going to make the 1982 season into a fiasco for me. I wasn't absolutely sure though, and therefore I didn't want to burn any boats at that point. That's why I stated the following in an interview with *Het Nieuwsblad* newspaper: '*It reminds me of the old guard from the good old days with Demeyer, Pollentier and myself. Willems and Verlinden fit into that framework perfectly. With Sergeant as a classy young rider making it complete.*'

This vision of a return of the old guard did not last very long, however. In Frankfurt, for example, Willems and I were sharing the same room. He ordered a bottle of wine in my name. When I got back to the room in the evening he asked me, "Would you like a glass of wine Freddy?"

"No, not tonight," I replied.

What happened afterwards had been carefully planned in advance with Jossart. The bill, in my name, reached the management of Boule d'Or who concluded that Maertens had been drinking on his own again.

Before the start of the season there was a meeting at the sponsor's offices in which Willems, Driessens, Delabastita and I were asked to be present.

I rang Lomme, "Are the women invited as well?"

"No, no women," Lomme said.

When I went to Delabastita's office on the day and knocked on the door and went in, I saw that Leentje, Willems' wife was there. Although I had nothing personal against Leentje, I thought if she was there why wasn't Carine allowed to be? Therefore I demanded that Delabastita rang my wife and apologise to her. Fortunately he did so; otherwise I would have walked out there and then. All of this is to illustrate that even before a race in the 1981-82 season had been ridden, I had a sinking feeling.

That season my brother Marc, with my help, signed a contract with Boule d'Or and made his professional debut. He won't enjoy reading what is coming up but, to this day, I'm still convinced that if he had shown a greater strength of character, he would have been able to turn in much better performances. As extenuating circumstances for him I have to add that he only became a professional cyclist at a point when I was past my peak. If he had been born earlier I would have been able to assist him in word and deed. Just like me, Marc made his professional debut in the Criterium of the Westhoek. In 1976 he had come 2nd in the national championship for newcomers at Rapertingen behind the West Fleming, Eric Borra. Nothing has been heard of the winner since then, which once again just goes to show that if a rider isn't given the proper guidance, he can *burn himself out* in the youth categories before his time. I'll repeat what I said earlier: a rider must be able to stand on his own two feet when he makes the step up from the amateurs to the professionals and then he will get to know his own potential or limitations. A star among the amateurs will not necessarily make a team leader among the professionals. If a young rider like that gets the chance he must not let it go to waste, but he must also have the humility, after one season, to judge whether he has the ability to handle team leadership. Someone who may be used as an example in this context is Ronald De Witte. He realised that he wasn't the one to be team leader but by taking advantage of tactics within the team he was able to win important races on several occasions. The majority of first year professionals behave in exactly the opposite way. They walk around with big heads thinking that they can beat anybody and they are far too conceited. The box of pills and the syringe are never far away.

I went through the various youth stages with WSC Torhout, but my brother Marc joined the more modest outfit, the 'Kortrijkse Groeningespurters.' It is generally better to become a member of a bigger club even though higher standards are expected of a rider before he can take part in an inter-club race. I regard these types of races as very useful for newcomers and juniors, being good preparation for later. Most clubs are well run nowadays; at WSC Torhout, for example, the juniors are currently under the auspices of Michel Pollentier. In our time we could only have dreamed of getting advice from such a big name. The only thing which is a pity is that there is such a strong sense of envy between the teams.

After 1982 I took Marc twice with me to new teams. In 1985, however, he stood on his own two feet when Alain De Roo introduced him to Paul De Baeremaecker, the team manager of TeVeBlad. On 19th July 1985 he won his first race as a professional at De Panne and that turned out to be the first of a long sequence. With eleven wins that season, he finished third in the table of Belgian winners behind Eric Vanderaerden and Eddy Planckaert. It could be put down partly to the fact that he had joined a team that raced almost exclusively in Belgium but also partly to his growing maturity.

Marc Sergeant won the 1982 Ruta del Sol which had started on February 2nd. I was struggling to keep my weight down and certainly didn't give the impression that I was the reigning world champion. In the first two stages two team-mates had to wait behind for me as I was unable to keep up with the pace. During the third stage between Almeria and Aguilas I abandoned.

At the root of this below par performance and my miserable season in 1982 was my dissatisfaction with the arrival of Daniël Willems. Although I trained, it was without conviction. I know that it seems illogical for the holder of the rainbow jersey to take life too easily but if everything is getting on top of you as it was with me – i.e. my tax problems, not receiving the bonus I had been promised or the Fiat Panda and Bauknecht kitchen and so on – you start asking yourself what you are actually still riding for.

I'm not going to use all the receptions I was invited to during the winter as an excuse for being overweight. After the close season I was still troubled by excess weight but thanks to an intensive training programme it quickly disappeared when things got back to normal. This time, however, I did not make myself sweat enough because I was so annoyed with the way the bosses at Boule d'Or wanted to see Willems on the podium.

After Prague I only attended the same number of receptions as

I did after Ostuni in the winter of 1976-77 so that couldn't have been the difference. Admittedly, I did sometimes drink a glass too many at these functions but who hasn't? If one were to carry out a study into the number of total abstainers among the riders the results would sadly be very low. I know a particular famous ex-world champion from Belgium who often needed a few whiskeys and smoked strong cigarettes during his career. Nobody ever made a fuss about that though because his name didn't happen to be Maertens.

On one occasion I went to collect Willems in my car so that we could travel together to the Henninger Turm in Frankfurt. He saw two empty 25cl bottles of Gueuze beer in the back and that was enough for him to let Delabastita know afterwards. *'We found bottles of booze stowed in Freddy's car.'*

Even Driessens slowly began to be swept along by the Delabastita-Jossart way of thinking. It was certainly in his own interests as he earned good money at Boule d'Or, despite the fact that he would tell the whole world that he only took on the job of directeur sportif as a hobby.

The following, however, is a fine example to show that the opposite was true. One day we came back on the plane from a race at Montjuich where I had given up during one of the stages. Because of this, Lomme said, the organiser did not want to pay me. Once we arrived at Zaventem Airport Carine and I got into the car. Suddenly I said to Carine, "I've forgotten to arrange with Lomme when I have to go and see him tomorrow. He'll still be in the departure lounge, I should think. Will you just go and ask him while I wait here in the car?"

When Carine got there she saw Lomme in the company of a journalist, whose name I would rather not mention, sitting in a corner fiddling about with some money. The penny suddenly dropped: they were busy sharing out my money. Lomme was taken completely by surprise when Carine approached him and he tried to answer her nonchalently, although it was obvious that he was covering something up.

Delabastita had Driessens in his pocket completely. When Wilfried Van Cauwelaert, Lomme's solicitor who worked in former minister Chabert's practice, died a couple of years ago, Delabastita gained access to certain delicate files. He therefore knew more than Lomme really wanted him to and was able to manipulate him. That explains why Driessens once insisted that I put in writing that I would not be taking any further legal action against Delabastita following his stunt with the publicity contract between the cake firm Vranckaert and me. I wouldn't hear a bad word said about Wilfried Van Cauwelaert though. On the contrary, if he had still been alive many of my problems would not have reached the gigantic proportions that they were to later.

Driessens leaving me to my own fate was exactly what Willems wanted. Later on they often talked about the Maertens-Willems-De Wolf triumvirate in the press. I used to (and still do) get angry whenever I saw that, as I simply can't understand why those two are mentioned in the same breath as me. What did they ever achieve?

Let me talk about my so-called *drink problem*. I admit that during that period when I was up to my neck in tax problems (and they got worse after 1982), I looked for consolation in a good strong drink. Sometimes instead of having a glass or two of wine with a meal I would drink the whole bottle. Carine would say at the time, "That's no solution Freddy. Your problems won't have disappeared tomorrow." She was right, of course, but what I did was only human. I have never felt like an alcoholic but just a social drinker. Everything seemed to be against me and the drink provided a form of escape. Anyway, I've had to carry a reputation as a boozer with me throughout my career. When Briek Schotte was still the directeur sportif at Flandria, the riders used to drink a glass of wine with their meals with the knowledge of supremo Paul Claeys. My notorious reputation as a drinker, however, dates back to when I won my first world title in Ostuni and twice signed a publicity contract with the French company, Lanson, in exchange for a thousand bottles of champagne. The fact that I sold a large number of the bottles to Briek Schotte among others was of little interest to the public. As far as they were concerned Maertens was on the champagne from nine in the morning.

Drink was certainly not the main reason for my slump in 1982. There was the underlying background that things were strongly amiss in the team between the management and me. For example, I could have ridden in the Six Day events at Antwerp, Rotterdam and Milan but was not given permission by Boule d'Or. That was just at a time when I could have really used the money for the tax people. Was it any surprise then that I couldn't

154

become motivated for the Ruta del Sol?

Willems was already complaining during the season's opening weeks about the lack of support in the Boule d'Or team, but as world champion what was I supposed to say? Nothing. Jossart made sure that all the other riders eventually took Willems' side. During the course of the season, Willems also demanded the outright team leadership for himself with the threat that if he did not get his way he would be seeking employment elsewhere.

26 Unsportsmanlike conduct

After the Ruta del Sol Lomme and I were given an audience with the Pope. We were in Palermo in Sicily and on that same evening I was supposed to be in Brussels to receive my Sportsman of the Year award, but first of all we were going to make a detour via Rome. We were picked up at the airport by the organiser of Tirreno-Adriatico who had organised the audience for us. When we arrived at the Vatican a mass was being held, led by the Pope, and we were to go right to the front. We had been granted a special pass for this. Before you could get it, your past had to be investigated to make sure you were not a bandit. (According to Vatican standards Lomme Driessens was not a bandit. Let's make that clear once and for all.)

When the mass was over the pope walked along the aisle shaking hands and letting people kiss the ring on his finger.

"Who does he think he is?" Lomme complained, expecting the Holy Father to come and greet us first. "Let's get going."

We stayed, though, and the Pope eventually came to us. I gave him my rainbow jersey and in turn received four blessed paternosters from him. From our conversation it was apparent that he was aware that I was a double world champion. I also told him that I had an aunt who lived at Olsztyn in Poland and that I wanted to get an aid programme underway for her village. Later this plan came to fruition. The caretaker of my supporters club took the articles of clothing and foodstuffs there in a lorry.

Following the audience we were taken back to Leonardo da Vinci Airport in Rome. Instead of ordering direct tickets to Brussels, Driessens had booked for Rome-Milan-Brussels. There are two airports in Milan, Linate and Malpensa, and the idea was that we were to land at Linate where we would then change on to another plane. However just before we were due to land, the passengers were informed that due to thick fog we would be landing at Malpensa instead. As soon as we had set foot on land I suggested to Lomme that we ought to take a taxi to Linate to make sure we didn't miss our flight.

"No, *comrade,* we'll go and have a bite to eat first," came the reply.

Of course we arrived too late at Linate. In the meantime they

Having become world champion at Ostuni in 1976, Maertens turns in a performance worthy of the rainbow jersey in winning the Grand Prix des Nations invitation time trial in 1977.
(*Photosport International*)

The finish of the infamous 1977 Tour of Flanders. Maertens
trails in behind Roger De Vlaeminck, a victim of the notorious
bike-changing incident referred to on pages 86-87.

The morning of 28th May 1977 at the Autodromo Mugello during the Tour of Italy. Maertens takes the sprint by a wheel from compatriot but deadly rival Rik Van Linden and the Italian Marcello Osler. (*Associated Press*)

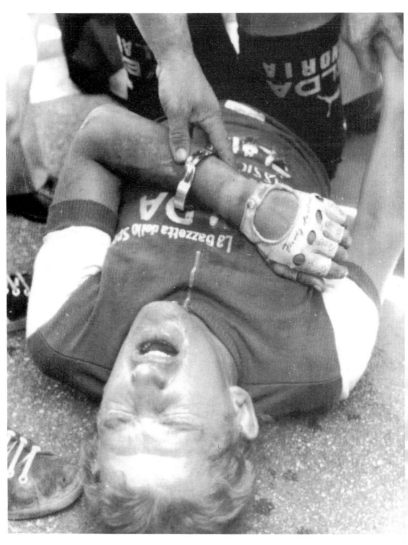

Maertens' 1977 Giro is over following a fall in the afternoon's sprint finish, once again involving Rik Van Linden. In spite of the broken wrist he receives in the crash, he still hopes to continue the race before having to concede that the injury is too serious.
(*Press Association*)

Maertens – in the green jersey – collects his 5th stage win of the 1981 Tour de France, on the Champs Elysées. A new generation of sprinters, Sean Kelly, Fons De Wolf (2nd on the stage) and Jean-Louis Gauthier witness the return of his legendary sprint power at close hand. (*Press Association*)

Later in the 1981 season and the icing is on the cake. At Prague, Maertens' second world title is under his belt. In the sprint he edges out Giuseppe Saronni and Bernard Hinault.

On the podium a look of pride disguises the feeling of happiness after the medal presentation.

The latter stages of Maertens' career saw him adorning the colours of a succession of lesser teams. Here he is seen in discussion before the start of Kuurne-Brussels-Kuurne in 1984 in an AVP-Viditel jersey. (*Photosport International*)

Freddy's last two seasons as a professional were spent riding for the modest Robland team. (*Photosport International*)

were waiting for us in Brussels for the Sportsman of the Year presentation. However in the end it couldn't take place that night and the presentation of the trophy had to be put back to another evening, at the offices of Boule d'Or.

It was nearly eleven o'clock in the evening when we finally touched down in Brussels.

"It's all your fault!" said Lomme.

Carine and Maria had been waiting for us all the time in the arrival lounge. Lomme insisted that my wife and I should stay the night at their house but I said that I had left a pair of shoes at home in Lombardsijde that I would be needing the following day when we returned to Palermo. What actually eventually happened was that Carine and I stayed the night at the Novotel near the airport as I really wanted to be alone with my wife on my birthday. The next morning Lomme and I set off early for Sicily, once again via the route that Lomme had booked – Brussels-Milan-Rome-Palermo.

In spite of all this, Lomme had shown a glimpse of his great organisational talent when it came to aeroplane flights on the eve of the Tour of Spain in 1977. Every team was stuck at Madrid Airport as a result of a pilots' strike. The original plan was that we would fly from Madrid to Dehesa de Campoamar where the prologue was to be held, but that was now out of the question of course. The event organiser then came up with a plan whereby everybody was to be ferried to the starting point of the tour by bus.

"Lomme, if you want me to set a good time in the prologue, try to *arrange* some different way of getting there, for heaven's sake," I said.

After a bit of thought he once again came up with a stunt which bore the Driessens trademark through and through. He suggested to the organiser: "Hire a private jet to fly the team leaders from each team to the prologue together." After an hour of discussion the deal was agreed. Driessens had of course handled it in such a way that Flandria were also allowed to take Demeyer and Pollentier. The other riders were also all for it as they saw the prologue purely as an obligation.

Yes, I remember planes well. After the stage from Beringen to Hasselt in the Tour de France of 1981, everyone was taken by bus to the military airfield at Brustem where a Sabena aircraft was waiting. The start of the following day's stage, an individual time trial, was a fair distance away in Mulhouse. Travelling on the plane were the tour director, all the riders, the directeur sportif and one physio from each team. The rest of the personnel made the transfer in the team cars. That day we flew into thunderstorms like I have never seen before or since. The aeroplane's wings were flapping up and down and the contents of the duty-free shop were flung everywhere. Even the stewardesses, who you would have thought would have to face situations like that all the time, were panicking. At a certain moment there was a sudden crack, a stewardess was sent flying on to our seats and she looked as white as a ghost. Alain De Roo grabbed her firmly.

"Hold on to me tightly and please don't let me go!" she cried to him, terrified.

Even Lomme, who normally took things in his stride, was sitting very sheepishly.

If this aeroplane had crashed, one of the Planckaert brothers would have become the overall winner of the Tour de France as they would never fly, and to this day still travel to races outside Belgium by car.

I didn't take part in the 1982 season's opener, Het Volk, as a result of the tribulations within the Boule d'Or team. Just before the prologue in Tirreno-Adriatico, Willems and I were warming up behind the team car which Lomme was driving. When an Italian driver signalled that he was coming out of a sidestreet onto the main road, Lomme slammed his brakes on as hard as he could, forgetting that we were right behind him. Willems was just able to avoid colliding with him but I hit the luggage carrier and was dragged thirty metres. I rode the prologue in a battered state and finished 133rd. I didn't finish that Tirreno-Adriatico or Milan-San Remo.

The 9th place I achieved in the Three-Days at De Panne was a bright spot for me. I was riding there in the service of Daniël Willems.

"You'll be amply compensated later for doing that," Lomme assured me. Three days after the final stage in the Three Days of De Panne, I was knocked over by a car during the Tour of Flanders.

We prepared for the Ardennes classics by riding in the Tour of

158

the Midi-Pyrenées, an event which was organised by Jacques Esclassan. The organisation *stank,* I have to say. The competitors had to sleep in schools and eat poor quality food in large halls where teams were only separated from each other by thin partitions. That year, hotel accommodation had been arranged for team leaders and managers only. That was supposed to be a favour, but one which was totally wrong in view of the far from comfortable conditions that the rest of the team had to put up with. When one rider went to the toilet in the middle of the night, he woke up all the eighty other riders at once. That is why I said to Lomme, "I'm staying with the others." Eventually, though, I was forced to join him and Willems.

A few days before Liège-Bastogne-Liège, Driessens arrived with a doctor at the room Willems and I were sharing and introduced him to us.

"This doctor is just going to examine your pulse rate and measure your blood pressure," we were told by Lomme.

That was, however, only a red herring for the real reason for his visit as I knew there was absolutely no problem with my blood pressure. I was under the medical supervision of Dr Derluyn and he had repeatedly told me, "I can't work out what's wrong with you. Physically there's nothing wrong at all."

Then the dark truth emerged.

"Listen," said Lomme. "This is the doctor in charge of the dope control tomorrow and you two can take whatever you like."

The doctor confirmed that he would turn a blind eye to anything we had taken.

"You both know how to go about it, don't you?" was his rhetorical question.

It was the first time I had met this man so when he had gone I said to Willems, "Do you think we can trust him?"

"Oh yes, definitely," replied Willems. "I know him."

"There's no need to worry," chipped in Lomme.

The following day, during Liège-Bastogne-Liège, I almost perished with the cold. The difference in temperature between the Ardennes and the Midi-Pyrenées was just too great. Putting another jersey on didn't help and so I retired. In the municipal swimming baths where the dressing rooms were located and the dope cointrol took place, I checked to see if my name was on the list of riders who were required to report. And of course I had been invited to this *reception*. Normally this would have been a formality in view of what had gone on the day before but when it came down to it it turned out that the doctor responsible for the dope control was different from the one I had spoken to the day before.

"What happens now?" I asked Lomme.

"Well, you're going to have to get out of this one yourself," was the only advice that came my way.

There I stood, then, made to look a complete idiot.

Fortunately I managed to get myself out of that scrape. The exact way I did it is of no consequence here. All I will say is that the way in which cheating the dope controls has developed in recent years has not only become greatly perfected but also more painful.

Daniël Willems did not have to provide a sample. Yet if I had have been found positive it would have given Boule d'Or sufficient grounds to give me the sack.

In Paris-Roubaix I was riding well until I fell on a cobbled stretch and smashed my chest onto my handlebars. My breath was cut off completely, something which was extremely painful.

On 1st and 2nd May I started in Frankfurt and Zurich respectively. In the Championship of Zurich I was *stabbed in the back* somehow (something dodgy was put into my food probably), as I was feeling extremely abnormal as I was riding. When I arrived home that evening I was so hyperactive that I couldn't get to sleep. I have to be eternally grateful that I wasn't called to the dope control that day. Since then I have always taken a Samsonite case with a combination lock with me to all races where a stopover is necessary.

Sandwiched in between all of my retirements in kermesse races after Zurich was one good performance and it was at Wielsbeke where, just like the previous year, I came 3rd. Also just like the year before, the motivation was equally strong as I didn't want to retire in the town of Burgomaster Noël Demeulenaere, who had done so much to help me.

I was given my so-called 'last chance' to earn a ticket for the Tour de France by Boule d'Or in the Midi Libre and the Tour de l'Aude. In the Midi Libre I had already given up the ghost in the first road stage. Without my knowledge, it was decided that my place in the team for the Tour de France was to go to Patrick Versluys. This time a call to Driessens' wife Maria to try to change her husband's mind was to no avail.

I can hardly claim that this came as a surprise. My not going to the Tour was purely the climax of the conspiracy which had been going on against me within the team throughout the season. It seemed as though when I had become world champion in 1981 it had been against the wishes of my own sponsor. Assistant directeur sportif Willy Jossart played a major role in the dirty underhand opposition I had to contend with. At the end of the 1981 season, for example, a disc-wheeled bike which the team had received from the Italian cycle manufacturer, Ernesto Colnago, had suddenly disappeared. Of course I was viewed as the guilty party even though I had only ridden it once, during the opening part of the Tour stage between Beringen and Hasselt. It was purely by chance that I found out what had happened. They had sold the bike to the brother-in-law of former rider Marcel Vanderslagmolen who one day asked me if I had any spare tyres for the small front wheel. All of a sudden I realised what had happened. It was just as well, as Boule d'Or were intending deducting the value of the bike from my monthly salary. Late one Friday evening I rang company director Daniël De Gieter at his home. His daughter answered and she tried at first to get rid of me. When she finally passed me on to her father, I threatened to go and have a word with Ernesto Colnago in Milan if my monthly salary had not been paid into my bank account by the following Wednesday. De Gieter didn't hesitate for very long.

In the national championship at Tertre I retired from the race. My brother Marc literally tried to prevent me from doing so by riding alongside me as it was clear to him that I wasn't even having a bad day. In the hotel I had steak and chips with the proprietor, who treated me to a bottle of wine and I watched the rest of the race on the television.

After it had finished there was a meeting of the Boule d'Or riders, in which the ones who had been chosen for the Tour de France received their new bikes. Even though I realised that there wasn't going to be one for me, I took up position by the delivery van.

"Do I get my bike?" I asked the mechanic.

"You're not going to the Tour," came the reply.

I went over to Jossart.

"You're staying home," he snarled.

"Right, at last I know," I said. "I thought that you would have at the very least had the tact to inform me officially."

I went looking for Driessens to *thank* him, got into my car and drove home. That evening Lomme wrote off a new Peugeot by driving the whole way home on the motorway in third gear. The engine was scorched and covered in smoke to such an extent that Willy Verlé had to put in many hours of work afterwards to get it ready in time for the Tour. With Willems as team leader, hardly anything went right for Boule d'Or during the Tour de France. I myself only took part in three races during July. I stayed in with Carine and Romy and shut myself off from the outside world (and from journalists in particular). In order not to be accused of breach of contract, from the beginning of August I appeared at the start of all the races that the team management ordered me to. On most occasions, though, I slammed on my brakes after a few circuits.

In spite of everything, I was selected for the world championships at Goodwood in Britain. I had conceived a plan to request the BWB, as the reigning world champion, to leave me at home but Boule d'Or wouldn't allow it. On the Thursday before the title race I was due to take part in a kermesse race at Kortemark along with two other riders who had been picked for the Belgian team, Michel Pollentier and Eddy Vanhaerens, while the rest of the team were already staying in Goodwood. That evening Pollentier and Vanhaerens, together with their team manager, Florent Van Vaerenbergh, caught the plane for England. I didn't know they were going to do that and I only set off the following morning.

Boule d'Or had promised me that somebody would be waiting at Heathrow Airport to collect me but I waited there in vain. First of all I rang Carine to find out if anyone might have got in touch with her in the meantime, but discovered that was not the case. In the end I telephoned the Richmond Arms Hotel where the Belgian team was staying.

"Seeing as you travelled without the others, you'll have to sort it out for yourself how you're going to get here," was what Jossart said from the other end of the line.

I cashed a cheque to get some English money and tried more than twenty taxi drivers before I could find one who was prepared to take me such a long distance. Finally, a driver about fifty years old and who had heard of me, agreed to take me. We talked for a while and I fell asleep for about an hour in the back seat. It was a really hot day and the driver was sweating heavily so I suggested that we should stop at a pub somewhere so we could have a beer. Fred Daman, a journalist with the newspaper *Het Laatste Nieuws* found this to be sufficient reason to write that when I arrived at Goodwood I was half-cut. This was the Fred Daman who I had known since my younger days as, like me, he lived on the coast. One day he came to our house and Marc Demeyer happened to be there and together we had Fred drinking one glass of cognac after another until he was in such a state that we made him pump up no less than twenty-eight tyres in my garage.

"That was hard work!" he said to Carine when he came back in through the kitchen out of breath.

When I arrived at Goodwood in the taxi on Friday afternoon, I received a cool reception. Along with Pollentier and Vanhaerens, I went to familiarise myself with the course straightaway.

On the Saturday evening there was the incident involving the BWB doctor Daniëls. He didn't want to give me the *drip* with glucose and vitamins which Dr Derluyn had supplied as it had no label with a list of ingredients and instructions for use. Later he claimed that its milky consistency suggested to him that it was cortisone. My question is: would Dr Derluyn have been so stupid as to let a drip containing cortisone, a banned product, be infused by the federation's own doctor? The truth of the matter is that the accusation only followed from what had happened between us the year before in Prague. When he came to congratulate me on winning the title, I accused him of neglecting his duties and said that he could only be found when there was a party going on.

The story which Dr Daniëls had made up gained greater credence when, towards the end of the 1986 season, Dr Derluyn was brought into discredit by William Tackaert's public confession. He claimed that Dr Derluyn had been giving him cortisone regularly and that had led to his complete *downfall* as a cyclist. I found Tackaert's argument to be very weak, he had only visited Dr Derluyn on a few occasions and it was wrong to report it to the world as though he had been totally wiped out by him. Dr Derluyn treated me for a long time and I know better than most that he is a serious sports doctor who wants nothing to do with charlatans and riders who want to play the chemist themselves. That's why I always took Dr Derluyn's side throughout the Tackaert affair especially when he started to have problems with the Order of Physicians, something in which Dr Daniëls played no minor role.

When the Tackaert affair was in the news, archive pictures of me were shown on the television. Once again I had received some extra *publicity*. Why is it that when it is anything to do with doping, it is always the name Maertens and not the name Merckx, for example, which comes to the foreground? I suppose it's like Rik Van Looy once said to me, "As long as they talk about you it means that you're still interesting."

The to-do caused by Tackaert has to go down as being totally despicable. His actions were a real body blow to the world of cycling racing, which already has a bad enough image in comparison to other sports. That is why I immediately telephoned Dr Derluyn to offer him my support and also because he has always had a fair and impartial view of me. He once summed it up perfectly in an interview with 'De Morgen' newspaper:

'Maertens has been the victim of physical factors. He is not burned out. There has never been anything physically wrong with Freddy. You just had to talk to him for hours – to motivate him. Maertens wasn't sick, nor was he addicted to drugs. He just had mental problems which can be traced back to a lack of self-confidence. He has been blown out by cycling's mafia, not by the use of anabolics or cortisone.'

In Goodwood, where the rainbow jersey was to go to Saronni, I retired early in the race. Willy Verlé came into my room with the bottle of champagne that he otherwise would have emptied into my drinking bottle and we finished the bottle off together. It was like a bitter farewell toast to the final appearance in the last World Championship of my career.

27 Hearsay

During the winter of 1982-83 the air was buzzing once again with all sorts of rumours about my private life. Sometimes I would return home and say: "Carine, did you realise that at the moment you're running a chip shop in Middelkerke?" Or Carine would say: "Freddy, do you want to hear the latest news? I've heard that I'm a teacher at the Zon and Zee home." We never let all this gossip bother us that much. What did cause us sleepless nights, though, were our tax problems. They were frightening because they were our reality.

We often just had to laugh when yet another story about us surfaced, although sometimes I would wonder who it actually was who had made up the tale first. On one boiling hot summer's day, Carine was lying outside sunbathing. Robert *Blondie* Deramoudt looked after our garden and was watering the flowers. For a joke he suddenly pointed the hosepipe at Carine who had nodded off. She leapt to her feet in fright.

"You big bully!" she shouted as she ran away.

Blondie and I took up the chase, him with the hosepipe and me with a full bucket in my hand. Carine tried to escape and gave out a scream. A couple of weeks later the story was going round that I had been dragging my wife round by the hair and that she had been letting out terrifying screams.

On one occasion I got up in the middle of the night to go to the toilet when I happened to see our neighbours, Willy and Rosa Vandersteene, with whom we had a good relationship, arrive home.

I opened the window and, to their great surprise, they heard a voice coming out of the darkness saying, "Late home tonight, aren't we folks?"

Willy shouted something back and a childish sort of conversation developed between us. Some time later, when Carine was doing some shopping one day at his butcher's shop in Nieuwpoort, Willy said to her, "You probably haven't heard about it yet, but we are supposed to have had a huge row. A customer came into the shop to tell me that he witnessed a scene one night when all hell was let loose between us."

Through Marc Snoeck, who took my mother to the hospital

every week for her dialysis treatment, we were given a communion bench from the pastor of Ingelmunster as a present for our lounge. This bench, complete with beautiful sculptures, stood on the first floor of a youth centre and was situated at the top of the stairs to make sure none of them went tumbling down them. We could have it on the condition that we supplied them with a new balustrade. For that reason, for a few days, there were a number of planks of wood in front of our house. The conclusion which was drawn from that was quickly reached: Maertens had smashed his own furniture to pieces.

For anyone who wants to believe it, I also fired shots through our ceiling with my hunting rifle.

What woman do you think would put up with half of the things that I'm supposed to have done? This year (1988), Carine and I will have been married fifteen years. How many other couples can say they have lasted as long nowadays?

Carine managed to not let all the nonsense talked about us show on the outside. She found it more difficult with other things though, like whenever we received letters in which someone was threatening to throw paint at our house. She decided: "Imagine if one nutcase gets it into his head to do it one night and we're not at home . . ." The thing that frightened her most, however, was the fear that something might happen to Romy. My second world title victory in Prague made some people more jealous and, for fear of Romy being kidnapped, Carine told the staff at school to be extra careful she wasn't taken away by a stranger who claimed to be taking her home.

Although at first it was easy for me to dismiss the wild stories circulating about how I was mistreating Carine and Romy, eventually I felt as though everybody saw me as a criminal. That explains why I became very wary of people. It got so that I preferred to stay at home lounging around on the settee. Whenever we had been anywhere and Carine suggested stopping on the way for a coffee or a glass of beer I would say, "Not in this bar, there are too many people inside." To which Carine would answer, "Why not Freddy? You haven't murdered anyone!"

The truth of the matter was that with all my financial worries I preferred to be left in peace and quiet.

During all the difficult times, Carine and I were still able to preserve our relationship, in spite of what was said about us. As a

166

small family the three of us depended on each other, and for me that was the only motivation I needed to keep going. It was not unusual for Carine and me to sit talking until three o'clock in the morning (sometimes with my father there as well) and cheering each other up. Carine would say then, "Forget our money troubles and try to concentrate on your racing." I would keep trying to put this into practice but it failed every time. Anybody who has not lived through our financial nightmare – tossed backwards and forwards from tax claims to writs – would find it difficult to appreciate how low it makes you feel. In the wink of an eye you see all your hard-earned cash slipping through your fingers. Then you naturally ask yourself: what's the point of carrying on racing? Just to give everything back? That's how I continued – without hope – for another two years. If the Burgomaster of Wielsbeke, Noël Demeulenaere, hadn't begun to handle the legal side of my affairs, I don't know how we would have ended up. He deserves to have a giant golden feather stuck in his cap.

In those terrible days Carine was as solid as a rock when I was around. However as soon as I was away riding abroad, she suffered. At night she couldn't sleep through worrying and not being able to see an end to it all. Fortunately, as well as Noël Demeulenaere, we could also count on other friends. For example, hunt inspector Jef Muylle, who paid for my hunting licence himself and Raoul Bouve who gave us a great deal of help. With Jef, Raoul, *Blondie*, garage owner Roger Dombrecht and Milo De Néve, who had designed our villa, we once had a night to end all nights after a hunting party.

Apart from the couple already mentioned, Willy and Rosa Vandersteene, we also had some other good neighbours including André and Simonne Vandevelde from whom we had bought the land on which our house was built. There was also Michel Vanhee who seemed to be handy at everything, and his wife Lisette. Along with the painter and decorator, Lucien Nivelle, Michel did lots of little jobs for us.

All of the above are people who Carine and I will not forget in a hurry because of what they have done for us. There are others as well, too numerous to mention here. When you are in need you find out who your friends are, as the saying goes. It may be a cliché but what else can I say other than thanks to all of you.

167

On the sporting side of things, there was little for me to shout about in 1983. Through Albert Van Vlierberghe, I found myself a place in the team at Masta. Albert had been an old team-mate of mine at Flandria and had been managing the Masta team since 1982. The team leader was Johny De Nul, *the king of the kermesses.* He had also been a rider at Flandria but there had been great ructions during his time there. When Dirk Heirweg and he joined us straight from the amateurs they acted very arrogantly and demanded a protected role from the beginning. Obviously that didn't go down too well with Demeyer, Pollentier and me and the two dissidents were forced to toe the line of team discipline, with the result that they gave me the title of *big head.*

Over the years De Nul had calmed down and so there was nothing standing in the way of me joining Masta. I was signed for the task of helping him in important races. It didn't bother me that he carried the title of official team leader. Albert, meanwhile, gave me the impression that he was a talented directeur sportif who knew how to exercise his authority when it was necessary. The team, however, was too modest in scale to expect to achieve any great successes.

At Masta I received a monthly salary which was appreciably higher than the BF 30,000 I had to settle for in my first year at Boule d'Or. First of all TVS were to come in as co-sponsors and it was planned that there would be a pay rise for my brother Marc and me when the team became TeVeBlad. The latter part of the plan came to fruition before the presentation of the team had taken place, but we never did receive the BF 300,000 which had been promised us when the transaction took place. There is still a legal action pending regarding this money.

One of my main objectives was to play a prominent part in Ghent-Wevelgem. I prepared well for this *echelon race* which has always been close to my heart, but in the closing stages I suffered a flat tyre just before the climb of the Rodeberg. If that had not happened I would more than likely have found a place on the podium. Bernard Hinault and I tried in vain to get back up to the leading echelon. Photographs of our combined effort appeared in the newspapers accompanied by a caption along the lines of: *'Two riders in trouble,'* as Hinault was struggling at the time with tendinitis.

In the classics I didn't receive much support from my team-mates except for my brother. I rode them in exactly the way I would have had to as an amateur – on my own. I couldn't point an accusing finger at anyone, though. As De Nul had won a good many races the year before, it was to be expected that the others would be riding for him. In 1983, however, he had a poor season and as far as I was concerned, his main problem was that he lacked the stamina to break through the 200km barrier.

Two days before Ghent-Wevelgem, I won in Hannuit and this was to be my only victory of the whole season. It would have been more if there had been a greater sense of unity in the Masta team. For example, in Kalmthout, Marc and I rode in the leading group, yet guess which team closed the gap to us, the Mastas. It was, therefore, a similar state of affairs to that which had been going on at Boule d'Or. I fell out of the frying pan into the fire. When I realised this, it didn't really bother me, because as far as I was concerned, I was glad to wash my hands of it.

This scenario was played out again the following season. I always started every season highly motivated but through the various goings-on my enthusiasm faded quickly. In all honesty I have to add that I didn't always go flat out. A feature of a true champion is that it is precisely during these difficult times that he can grit his teeth and carry on; however for me that was no longer the case. Nevertheless, it seems that I was still enough of a draw for the public to be offered a contract by somebody every season. You see, even if I wasn't riding in a race, they would still be talking about me.

28   Goodbye dream home

I had already, in principle, signed a contract with Splendor for the 1984 season when the deal hit a snag. Their management refused to take on my brother Marc as well, so in the end the transfer never went through. I eventually signed for Jaak De Goede's Dutch team, AVP-Viditel. I was first put in contact with them through Jan Van Poeyer who worked for Beckers Snacks. Before a race in Hulste in 1983, Van Poeyer (who was still a rider at that time) and I were changing into our racing gear at Annie Monseré's house when he told me what his plans were for the following season. My arrival in the team meant that AVP-Viditel could increase interest in cycling sponsorship. For the first time in my career, I signed a contract which consisted of a monthly salary supple-
mented by a system of bonuses.

While Francesco Moser was twice breaking Eddy Merckx's world hour record in quick succession in January 1984, I was once again, full of good intentions, concentrating on the new season. In my first race of the season on 5th February, the Grand Prix of Malaga, which was only raced over a distance of 45 kilometres, I couldn't keep up with the pace and retired. Some riders were going flat out from the very start and although I had put in a fair amount of training, I was not up to the sudden acceleration needed to keep up. The Ruta del Sol began the next day and the first two riders to be left behind were the Maertens brothers. Fortunately I managed to get back up to the peloton and Marc arrived within the time limit as well.

That evening De Goede came to my room, "Freddy, tomorrow is a difficult stage. Make sure you have a go, won't you!"

"Of course," I replied. "Isn't that what I was doing today?"

The next day, I had to drop off the back on one of the climbs and was on my way back up to the group when I was hit by a motor-bike. Annie Monseré and her husband Marcel, who were on holiday in Spain, had hired a car so that they could follow the Ruta del Sol from close by. They never saw me pass them though, and it is hardly any wonder as I was sitting in the broom wagon.

From March onwards, neither De Goede nor Van Poeyer were bothered about me any more. I had served my purpose for them by attracting sponsors to the team with my name, and in that they were successful. Apart from that, I was of no use to them. The type of person Jaak De Goede is was illustrated a few years later when he was arrested in London accused of trafficking in narcotics.

On 3rd April, I received a letter of dismissal by registered post. I have no idea how they felt they had the right to do that as the very most they were entitled to do was to fine me. Needless to say, the BWB did nothing to contest my sacking. The reason they gave was that it was beyond the jurisdiction of the Belgian Cyclists Federation as AVP-Viditel came under the auspices of the Royal Dutch Cycling Union (KNWU). If that is so, why is it that both the BWB and the KNWU are both members of the UCI, the International Cycling Union, the sport's co-ordinating body? Is it simply so that the gentlemen can wear matching jackets? Once again, Sporta failed to do anything and gave me no active legal assistance whatsoever.

Burgomaster Noël Demeulenaere helped me to get a two-month trial contract with Splendor, but I only wore their colours on a couple of occasions. I was not on the same wavelength as the team-manager, Albert De Kimpe, and I never received any of the money due to me. Before the start of the prologue to the 1985 Tour of Belgium, I happened to notice De Kimpe and rode up to him.

"What's happened to that money you still owe me?" I asked.

"What's happened to that bike that you got from us?" was the question he replied with.

"It's been sold!" I said.

"Don't you think it's a crying shame that you're so ungrateful after everything that *Mr. Noël* has done for you." he moaned.

"There's obviously a big difference between the way *Mr. Noël* conducts his business with the way you do things at Splendor." I said, and that shut him up.

I worked in my father's cycle shop, alongside my brother Luc, until the end of the tourist season. While Luc was busy carrying out repairs, I sold new bikes. My working day began at around half past seven in the morning when I had to put the bikes and advertising boards outside. The news quickly spread that I was working there and I managed to sell an average of two cycles a day to visitors to the coast. One day, a German couple came into the shop and I sold a bike to both the man and the woman. In the afternoon they came back with their three children and another three bikes found new owners.

On another occasion I almost lost a potential customer. He wanted to buy a particular bike but the saddle was not right for him. I had brought out all the other types of saddle and fitted them on the bike but it appeared that none of them seemed to suit him. I was gradually getting really tired of this, so after half an hour I finally said to him, "There's only one more saddle that might be of use, it's the one that was originally intended for my own racing bike."

I went into the sitting room and after taking a quarter of an hour to drink a cup of coffee, picked up the first saddle I saw lying around in the back and showed it to the customer.

"I must add straightaway that it is a special type and, because of that, it will cost a couple of hundred francs more," I said while trying to keep a straight face.

"Fantastic!" the man replied. "It feels as if it was made for me."

And that's how that bike was sold.

During this period there was a terrible accident involving my mother. One morning Carine and I arrived at the shop a bit later than usual when suddenly I got a phone call from some neighbours of my parents.

"Freddy, you must come rightaway. Something has happened to your mother."

My father and my brother Luc were out at the time delivering newspapers. We rushed to my parents' house and could hardly believe our eyes when we got there. In the shop was a huge pool of blood, just as if someone had had their head chopped off. What had happened? My mother had wanted to move a moped and while she was in the process, her calf got caught on the machine and an artery was severed. Due to the fact that she was undergoing dialysis twice a week, her blood was very thin and because of that, it literally *spouted* out. Forunately, the neighbours had already called for a doctor and when he arrived he not only needed to treat my mother but me also, since when I had seen what had happened, I fainted.

On Friday 28th December 1984 we moved out of our villa in Westende. We had tried to put off selling it for as long as possible but now it was unavoidable. We had been bled dry by the tax office and as soon as we had no reserve capital left in our bank account to pay off our debts, we had no other option. Having to give up the dream home which we had had built for ourselves from our own money (the structural work alone cost 8 million francs), caused us a great deal of pain.

That Friday morning it was as if we had been nailed to the ground when we watched the new owners moving in with a whole team of helpers. Christine (Carine's sister) and Christa came to help us pack everything away and put our furniture in the garage. They seemed to be upset by it all as well. When we saw how everything was being completely changed in the villa which used to be ours, Carine and I sat in the garden shed crying like two small children. The following day Carine had to ring the new owners to ask if they would ever so kindly let us have one or two things from the garage. Only two days earlier we had been lord and master there.

Our dog, Flits, a dobermann pinscher, stayed in the villa. Romy was very sad that we had to do this and I felt the same way, but how could we have possibly managed with him when we moved into our new apartment in Nieuwpoort, after living at my parents for two months? I still have Flits' certificate of pedigree and still think of him as our own dog.

We tried to avoid visiting our ex-neighbours as much as possible so that we wouldn't have to face seeing our old villa. One day we were invited round by Willy and Rosa Vandersteene and so I used it as an opportunity to go and have a look at Flits. He recognised me straightaway and enthusiastically jumped up at me. Just at that moment, the woman who was now living in our house arrived home.

"I've just come to say hello to Flits," I told her.

Later on I discovered that she had intended to make out a complaint against me *because I had wanted to steal her dog.*

29 I am a Junkie

In November 1984 I was reunited with Lomme Driessens for the second time. It was, nevertheless, after some hesitation on his part. Once again it was his wife, Maria, who had talked him into giving me a third chance. The directeur sportif of the new team which was formed around me was Jos Elen from Elro-Snacks who had brought in the company Nikon as the main sponsor. The very well-organised, though expensive, team presentation took place in an hotel somewhere near Amsterdam and all the riders were ordered to be there a couple of days beforehand. When the journalists and other guests were leaving, they received a surprise gift which was a bag containing, among other things, a bottle of spirits. Suddenly it appeared that there weren't enough bags as some people had gone off with more than one. In view of my reputation as an alcoholic, I decided it would be a wise move to give my bottle to a team-mate.

Driessens was given the title of team *supervisor*. During the winter he regularly visited me at our flat in Nieuwpoort and I did what he asked me, just as I had done in two previous stages of my career. It wasn't that I was expecting to make a sensational comeback after Prague, but it was the last straw at which I could clutch. At least I was in a team again and with Driessens I knew where I stood. For that reason, I listened to him just like a child to its father and followed all his instructions to the letter. I resolved to become a worthy professional rider again in 1985 and I thought Lomme would be there to help me. On the eve of Milan-San Remo, it became clear to me that it had all been an illusion.

Milan-San Remo took place on 16th March. On the previous Monday, I was due at Lomme's home in Vilvoorde by four o'clock in the afternoon so that, with Frank Verleyen, we could then go to Venlo, in the Netherlands, where the whole team was to spend a few days training for Milan-San Remo. Because I was half an hour late arriving at Lomme's house, due to the fact that my father had taken the car to the garage for a service and it had taken longer than expected, he gave me a real mouthful when I arrived.

When Carine and I were saying goodbye to each other in Vilvoorde, she said to me, "Freddy, watch out, there's something going on. This isn't the same Lomme I used to know."

She could always see through people more quickly than I could. As far as Lomme was concerned, his job was done. The contracts with the sponsors had been signed, the team had been put together, his money had already been earned so what was left for him to do?

Lomme and I went to pick up Frank Verleyen and Carine stayed with Maria for a while.

"Don't worry, Lomme is just a little tense," Maria said.

Carine, however knew better.

In Venlo we trained on the Amstel Gold Race course. While we were approaching the hotel after a team training session, Frank Verleyen and I collided with each other and we both went crashing to the ground. I was left with two knees swollen with blood and fluid from this crash. Lomme, however, thought that there was no need to call in a doctor. He instructed my physio, *Sjef* Van Lommel, to see what he could do. *Sjef* put ice on my knees and the result was that they turned blue and green as well.

"What's the point of my travelling to Milan-San Remo," I said to Driessens. "I can hardly stand up, so I might as well go home."

"Oh no you're not. You're coming to Milan-San Remo with the rest of us," Lomme replied, using the argument that the team wouldn't receive any money if I didn't show up.

On the Thursday afternoon we set off in three cars rather than an aeroplane for Milan. We stopped about forty kilometres short of the city centre.

"This looks like a good place to stay overnight," said Lomme, as he hadn't booked an hotel.

The next day, after a light training session, we went to collect our numbers for Saturday's race. In the evening I asked, "What time are we getting up tomorrow?"

Because we were staying so far away from where the race was to start, the very thing I feared would happen, did so the next morning. Everything had to be done in a mad rush. I only had one of my legs massaged, while other riders had to make do without a massage at all. Despite all the rushing around, we still arrived at the start late. The peloton had already set off and so right from the beginning we had to start chasing in the pouring rain.

I dropped out of the race after a little more than thirty kilometres. Lomme pulled up alongside me in the team car and I told him that I would start making my way back to the motel. An Italian spectator took me back to his house where he let me have a wash and lent me a tracksuit. He then took me to the hospital in Pavia. The doctor gave me a couple of pain-killing injections for my knees, an infiltration was carried out to absorb the water and blood, and they treated the injury to my little finger which was also a result of the crash with Frank Verleyen. They wanted to detain me in the clinic but I refused and had to make out a written declaration that leaving the hospital was my own responsibility. We went back to the Italian's house where we ate before the kind man finally took me back to the motel.

When the other riders arrived back from San Remo, I was lying in bed. Nobody woke me for the evening meal. Driessens opened the door to my room and could see that I was sleeping. He went to tell the others that I was in a dazed state and that at long last he knew the real reason for my peculiar behaviour: *"Maertens is addicted to drugs."*

In the morning *Sjef* banged on my door and shouted, "Get up and put your things in the car, we're going now."

I had no time to have any breakfast. Frank Verleyen informed me what Lomme had announced behind my back the night before. Frank and I had shared a room in Venlo and therefore he didn't attach a grain of truth to what had been said. However, since he was still only a first year professional, the others were naturally more inclined to fall for Lomme's eloquence and conviction than believe him.

I put my case in the car and my bike went on the roof rack. Lomme didn't say a word to me, neither did team-manager Elen and even *Sjef* no longer spoke. I found myself travelling in the car with team-mates Peter Van De Knoop and Martin Kemps who had both had a good time the previous evening and now had hangovers. I could see that Lomme was in the car in front of us making emphatic gesticulations amidst a haze of cigar smoke. I could tell that it was something to do with me and that there was something afoot. When we had gone some distance, I asked Kemps:

"Have you counted how many riders there are in the three cars altogether?"

"No," he answered surprised.

"Go on then, count them," I said.

It turned out that we had left Frank Verleyen behind at the motel.

Carine and the rest of the riders' wives were waiting for us at the home of Frits Berghmans, the team's public relations officer. When we arrived there I indicated that I wanted to get my bike from the car but I was stopped by the mechanic.

"I've been ordered to hang on to your bike," he said.

Driessens and Elen called Carine into the kitchen to see them.

"We feel it would be better if you told Freddy you thought he shouldn't ride any more," Lomme told her.

"Why, what's happened?" Carine asked.

"Well he certainly won't be riding for our team any more. We've found out something that we didn't realise before. Freddy isn't addicted to amphetamines but to hard drugs."

"That's impossible!" cried Carine. "In the first place, where would we get the money from to buy them? And secondly, if that were true, don't you think I would have realised it myself?"

They maintained, however, that it was true. Carine angrily left them and came back to me. On our way back to Belgium that was the only thing we talked about. Lomme had found the stick he needed to beat me.

Once home, I went to see Dr Verhelst, taking with me the medical certificates I had been given at the hospital in Pavia. I had also shown them to Lomme but he doubted that they were genuine. To me that showed he could no longer see reason and that he wanted me out at any price.

On the Wednesday morning after Milan-San Remo, I was ordered to report to the BWB doctor, Dr Dirix, in Sint-Niklaas. However, Carine only found the telegram with the instructions in the post-box that afternoon, making it impossible for me to make the appointment. I phoned Dr Dirix, offered my apologies and we fixed a new time and date. Until such time as I had undergone the tests my professional licence was to be withdrawn. I am the only rider in the history of Belgian cycling who has ever been made to prove that they were medically fit to carry out their profession in the middle of a season.

I took Carine with me to all the examinations I had to undergo, including this one in the clinic at Sint-Niklaas. I wanted her to see what they did, such as the test on the bike with electrodes on my head and the examination of my blood; in short, everything. I demanded her presence so that the gentlemen of the BWB could not declare me to be completely *crazy*. Yes, they tried that once. By withdrawing my licence they intended to put an enormous psychological burden on me.

The final test took place in Professor Debackere's *veterinary science* laboratory in Ghent. The professor was not there himself and one of his assistants gave me a pot normally used for horses into which I had to give a urine sample.

"Where will my urine actually be sent?" I asked. "The container hasn't been sealed so anything might happen to it."

"Mr Maertens, everything has been done correctly," the assistant answered. "There won't be any funny business here."

"I hope you're telling the truth, because a lot depends on this for me," I said. "I'm being deprived of my livelihood, and I don't want it to continue because of my being wrongly accused of taking drugs."

When I first went to see Dr Dirix, I had to make a written declaration stating that I bore him no personal malice and that I would not take any legal action against him. He knew only too well which way the wind blew.

As soon as these examinations were completed, Carine and I were summoned to his house. All the results were favourable and nothing was found in my urine. It seems that my only problem was that I was a little overweight.

Sometime later we were asked to attend the clinic at Sint-Niklaas where we would receive the neuropsychologist's report.

"There is absolutely nothing at all wrong," he informed us.

"Everything is normal," after which he asked Carine, "What do you think about that, madam?"

"Well doctor, I just don't know what sort of game they've been playing at our expense." she replied.

How is it, then, that the BWB didn't win an outright victory over me at the time? It is because Professor Debackere was the stumbling block. He would never stray from his principles. Nothing had been found in my urine and so he made out a report to that effect. But more than that, he actually took my side and unfortunately that was to cost him dearly later. That partly explains the fact that since then the BWB have only found it necessary to use the laboratory of Professor Heyndrickx and not Professor Debackere. I am one hundred percent certain that he was put under pressure to give a negative result on me in 1985. The fact that he didn't yield to blackmail does him great credit. I will repeat then what I've already said in this book: Professor Debackere is someone who maintains high standards and who is, above all, an honest man.

It took quite a time before I got my licence back from the BWB. In the meantime I had collected all the doctors' bills together, put them in a large envelope and sent them to the Federation. They were wise enough not to send them back to me.

One afternoon I had to report to a meeting of the BWB's national sport committee in Brussels. The bigwigs sat at a long table with chairman Ernest De Vuyst in the middle and Aloïs Laperre, the then chief representative of West Flanders, formally present. I appeared just like a defendant before a court.

"Take your place," I was told. "The meeting is in session."

De Vuyst opened my file out in front of him, leafed through a few documents, looked me straight in the eye and said to me,

"Freddy, in future I hope you use your common sense a little more."

"What are you insinuating by that, Mr De Vuyst?" I asked.

"That if you don't act the way you ought, it will reflect badly on cycling in general."

"Mr De Vuyst, did the final medical report contain a positive or a negative conclusion."

"A positive one."

"Well then? I'm the only rider who has ever been required to justify myself in such a way in the middle of a season. Why is it that the rider happens to be Freddy Maertens again? I can assure you all of one thing: I still intend to carry on racing for a couple of years but the day I stop, I will no longer keep quiet."

I said all of this in an assured tone but I noticed that as I spoke everybody began to frown. I could tell that one or two of the members present, including the representative from Luxemburg province, basically thought I was right.

"And now I would like my licence please, gentlemen," I said.

When it was returned to me I just said, "Bon appetit! You can all go and have another free meal now." and left.

Thanks to Marcel Vanhoutte, Annie Monseré's partner, who

knew one of the directors of Euro-Soap, Mr Hoste, I signed a contract with the Euro-Soap-Crack team.

On Saturday 14th July 1985, in the programme *Le Magazine* on the French television station Antenne 2, they showed how Michel Galloo and Gisèle Bossuyt from Comines had been to my house practising exorcism. Lomme had met them at the velodrome in Ghent and introduced them to me.

"I've finally found the people who will be able to help you," said Lomme, and he arranged a meeting with them. When I heard that they were Roman Catholics, I immediately agreed to go along with it.

At the first meeting with them at our flat in Nieuwpoort, both Carine and I were treated. During one of these sessions, Gisèle would place her hands on my head and Michel would stroke the pressure points on my shoulders and back. While I was holding a crucifix in my hands, they would read a ritual based on the prayer of St.John. The first time and second time they did this I began to sweat profusely. Many people don't believe in God, but can it be denied that such a thing as Evil exists? Anyway, I am convinced that Michel Galloo and Gisèle Bossuyt have the gift of being able to drive evil out of a person's body. We still see each other once a week and every night I read a text which they have given me: *The healing power of Jesus,* as a form of prayer.

Certain people had *manipulated* me out of jealousy. That is not superstition: it is possible to celebrate black masses in order to make the devil, Satan, enter somebody. I feel very good when Satan approaches me, "Come on then, have a go." He tries to tempt you in the same way as a woman is able to tempt you. I know no better way of expressing it. Other people may think of what Michel, Gisèle and I do as black magic but I have faith in them. They helped me overcome my depressive feelings of anxiety. Of course, they have a great laugh about all of this in the peloton. Sometimes they would mockingly shout, "Watch out, the devil's sitting on your back." I reacted to remarks like that by stating that the treatment I was receiving was a question of belief and that I didn't regard it as an amphetamine to help you win races.

I once had an intense discussion with the pastor of Lombardsijde who declared me to be mad. I had gone to see him to ask if he would come to my house to consecrate my bike.

"What sort of superstition is that!" he cried out. "Do you really think that that's the way you're going to win races?"

"That's not why I'm asking," I replied. "It's just that I don't want to ride a bike that hasn't been blessed."

And that was how it was. I quite simply felt safer riding a bike that had been consecrated. I can thank God that I was never left with any lasting damage from all the crashes I had.

I felt that the pastor's remarks were beneath contempt. Yet when I offered him a thousand francs, he eagerly accepted it. This has certainly not deterred me from continuing to attend the weekly mass. I like being with the fathers most of all because I feel as if I can be myself when I am with them. I am only against one of the church's institutions and that is confession. I prefer to tell God of my faults in silence rather than having to creep into the confessional.

On Thursday 11th July, which just happens to be Flemish national day, I won for the very last time in my career, at Gistel. I was part of the leading group and Ludo Frijns, who came from near my home and who was also a friend, and my team-mate, Alain Desaever, both said to me, "You must win here today."

I replied by saying that I had nothing left in me but they kept insisting.

"OK," I said. "But you two are going to have to share my prize money with me."

Eddy Vanhaerens, who at the time was still a team-mate of mine had, in the meantime, begun offering the others in the group a higher amount. That made me lose any interest in putting our plan into action. Then Alain Desaever became angry, "Freddy, you attack on the bridge over the canal. Ludo and I will go with you and ride at the front."

That's how it happened. On that day I was literally forced to win.

30 The day after tomorrow perhaps

In 1986 and 1987 I rode for the modest Robland team. Together with Noël Demeulenaere, who paid me each month, I was looking for sponsors in order to form a team. I made contact with the clothing firm Assos for the cycling clothes and Galli and Fietsen Conti for the equipment. Didier Paindaveine provided the team cars. All I wanted to do was to add a semi-classic to my honours list or to play a leading role in a race like Ghent-Wevelgem again, but nothing came of either of these ambitions. Afterwards it was easy for people to say that I should have retired at the end of the 1985 season. They shouldn't forget, however, that through my efforts a number of riders found a team for a couple of years.

The first race of the 1986 season in which our team wanted to compete was the kermesse at Blankenberge. Noël Demeulenaere had assured us that our registration money had been deposited in the BWB coffers and that we could therefore go and collect our licences. Five of us set off for the BWB's offices in Brussels. There, we were told by the administrative representative, Bijl, that one or two things still needed to be sorted out and that we would have to come back at another time.

"We've made this journey specially and I'm not going anywhere before I get my licence," I said.

"You definitely won't be getting it yet, you have to pass a medical examination first," Bijl replied.

"What? A medical examination?" I asked. "Do you want me to tell you something Mr Bijl. All the people who work in this building live off us, the riders."

I left the clerk looking perplexed and went down to the floor below, to the office of the chairman, Hector Gallée but he wasn't there.

"Come on Freddy, don't get so worked up," his secretary said, trying to calm me down.

Didn't I have the right to get worked up though, after everything the BWB had put me through the year before?

I telephoned Noël Demeulenaere and explained the situation to him. He demanded to speak to Bijl who immediately changed his tune. Everything had suddenly been settled. Once he had put down the receiver he said however, "It's already ten past five and the licences still have to made out. You'll all have to come back another time anyway."

"I want my licence now!" I replied. "If need be I'll sleep here on the carpet tonight and eat the goldfish from the aquarium."

I never had to follow up my threat though. I was able to make a start on the 1986 season but it didn't produce any highlights.

I prepared for the 1987 season in February in Spain. Carine and I were able to go free of charge with Annie Monseré and her husband Marcel to Torremolinos, where we stayed at the Hotel Pedro. It was certainly not the sort of holiday where I wanted to lounge around as I went training every morning and afternoon, sometimes in the company of riders from the Gewiss-Bianchi team who were staying nearby.

It was around three o'clock in the morning when we arrived back from Spain at our home in Rumbeke. Under the door was a letter from our directeur sportif, Luc Landuyt, telling me I was required to attend team training the next day. I didn't make it, though. In the afternoon I rang Noël Demeulenaere and explained to him that we had arrived home extremely late. A couple of days later there was another team training session. Luc Landuyt gave the other riders a signal to go flat out so that I would be dropped, but they were all astonished when they saw that I could comfortably stay the pace. Since I had lost a few excess kilos in Spain I felt really sharp. I had already decided, however, that this was going to be my last season.

At the team presentation at the Hippodroom Hotel in Waregem, my old boss Paul Claeys was present. It wasn't because he intended making a return to cycling, but because he had been helping in the search for new sponsors so that the team could be enlarged. If Jean de Gribaldy hadn't died around that time, our mission would probably have been successful. That very same day, in Waregem, I received a medal of merit from Tour de France assistant director, Albert Bouvet, for my performances in the Tour. I felt very honoured by this recognition.

I wanted to retire from cycling with dignity but a damper was quickly thrown upon my good intentions. While Noël Demeulenaere was abroad, Luc Landuyt and Patrick Decocq left me out of the team for the Three Days of De Panne. It was then that I said to myself, "That's enough! Did I put in all that work during the winter for this?" After the Circuit of the Flemish Ardennes at Ichtegem, I didn't start in another race in Belgium. Landuyt rang the BWB to have them block my monthly wages but, thanks to Noël Demeulenaere, I was paid until the end of the year.

On a couple of occasions I rode in Scotland with some of the riders from our team. That is how I slowly wound myself down, as to have stopped riding suddenly would have been bad for my heart. I had been put onto the contracts in Scotland by Mike Bennett from the media company 'Sport for Television'. It was also thanks to him that I was able to take part in the Kellogg's races in England in 1986. These races, which lasted one hour plus one lap, attracted riders of the quality of Stephen Roche and Sean Kelly. They were extremely popular in England and ITV television even broadcast them live.

The very last race of my career was the Fausto Coppi Race at Cuneo in Italy on 18th July 1987. I was not to be seen at kermesse races in Belgium either in my civvies or in the team car as, according to BWB regulations, if you are still the holder of a licence, you are not allowed to follow any cycling races from close by. I once rode as a pillion passenger on a motorbike in Paris-Brussels hidden under a huge crash helmet. Nevertheless, I was still recognised and received a large fine which fortunately was paid for by the newspaper *Het Laatste Nieuws* who had organised the stunt.

I received an offer to become directeur sportif of a Belgian team in 1988 but Carine didn't really want me to. If it had been just my decision I would have probably have accepted. That is because I never tire of cycling even though the mentality within the sport in the fifteen years that I was a professional changed completely. In the past we used to race against each other and then have a good chat afterwards, but that is no longer the case. I find it laughable because you have to be able to both win and lose. In my day, we would get together after a criterium and have a drink in each other's company. Now everybody goes their own way and there is no longer any sense of cameraderie.

I am now a representative for the sports clothing company, Assos, so I stay involved with the world of cycling in an indirect way, at least. I won the contract for the supply of clothing to the Isoglass team and almost managed it for François Lambert's ADR team until Frans Verbeeck, who is the distributor for another clothing make, put a spanner in the works. I will always have to fight and I'll always be ready to. I already have the agreement for the new team to be formed around Claude Criquielion for the 1989 season in my pocket.

I had been in contact with Assos, whose main office is at Pietro di Stadio in Switzerland, for quite a while, with a view to a job after my active career was over. While I was riding for Flandria I looked after the promotion of Assos clothing off my own bat and the management have never forgotten. When they were looking for an exclusive distributor in Belgium and Luxemburg I was given the first option. In a couple of years time I might also take in the Netherlands.

I'm my own boss and that suits me fine, since I have been self-employed all my cycling life. Business is good also. My name obviously helps and Assos will also have realised that. When I go to a place, I have no need to introduce myself, and that has helped sales. In the few months that I have been doing this job, I have learned one thing above all else and that is getting to know about people.

On 3rd July 1986, we moved into our present home in Rumbeke. By coincidence, this means that Carine has moved back to the village where she was born. We had asked her parents to keep an eye out for houses which they thought might suit us. It didn't matter which village it was in as long as it wasn't a flat, like the one in Nieuwpoort, or a house in the middle of a terrace. We found this one from an advert in the local newspaper, *De Streekkrant.* We really like it in this part of the village, De Vossemolen, where we have ideal neighbours in Joost and Martine. As long as the owners let us stay, we have no intention of moving.

Noël Demeulenaere has appointed a fiduciary solicitor who is looking into my financial affairs, as the taxation people are still after me because of the millions of francs I still owe them. In the not too distant future, the affair will be dealt with in the Supreme Court of Appeal. I hope things turn out favourably for me, but in the meantime it is a question of wait and see.

If everything had gone according to plan, I would now be a man of independent means or a gentleman farmer in France, but I don't feel any sense of bitterness when I look back at what's happened. You often hear people saying "If I could do it all over again, I would do things exactly the same." I say, "I would do it *differently*." I would certainly become a cyclist without a doubt, because I have always enjoyed cycling and it has often paid me very well. It's just a shame that the bookkeeping side of things got out of hand. But I don't regret anything else. I would just give one piece of advice to any young lad who is hoping to go a long way in cycling and that is; live for your job, because it is no easy matter. Also make sure you suffer more during training than in races themselves as that is the thing which makes the difference between winning and losing.

In the last few years I have repeatedly announced that this book would be written as soon as I gave up riding. Perhaps some people will find some of the sections harsh. It has not, however, been my intention to shock. I'm not someone who wants to dirty their own nest and I don't want to kick the profession to which I have much to be grateful. It is just that after everything that has been written and said about me in the past, I felt it was about time *my* version of events was heard. It is primarily because I am basically unable to do anything against injustice. Let me give you one final example. Eddy Merckx is one of the selectors of the Belgian team for the world championships, and that is quite logical as he has a great deal of experience and insight. On the other hand he has a vested interest and many of the riders ride on Eddy Merckx bikes. He is, therefore, both judge and plaintiff at the same time and that must cast doubt on the honesty of any selection.

Of course I have made mistakes during my life and I have been too gullible. However, in exchange for all the millions I have lost, I have found out who my real friends are, and that is a comfort to me. I also still have Carine and Romy, no-one has ever been able to take them away from me and that is more than a comfort, it is everything.

Now I take Carine, who in the past has had to spend a great deal of time without me around, with me every working day. We travel all around the country in our car which is packed full of sports clothing for the shops. Sometimes, as we are going through a little place, I will say, "Carine, I once won here, and look, over there, that's where we had to get changed." There would be a little nostalgia in my voice as I said it, I know. We often burst out laughing just like we were two small children, while at other times we sit silently next to each other letting our thoughts wander. On occasions while I'm driving I'll look at her and she notices and smiles and I'll smile back. I know what we have been through together and I dream that one day all our financial problems will be over. The day after tomorrow perhaps.

Is that called almost being happy?

Spring 1988

31 Postscript

It is now four years since this book was published in Belgium in its original Dutch form as *'Niet van horen zeggen.'* We felt, therefore, that for readers of the book in this, the English version, it was necessary to add this extra chapter to bring the story up to date. In order to do this we sought the views of Freddy Maertens – through co-author Manu Adriaens – on a range of subjects which we think anyone reading the book may want to know about.

The citation in the guidebook *"Dutch and Flemish Cycling Literature 1894-1990"* that *"Niet van horen zeggen"* was *'Of all cycling books, this one probably sold out its first edition faster than any other'* testifies to how much the book caught the imagination of the Belgian public. Manu Adriaens puts the reason not only for this, but also the fact it was so well-received, down to the fact that people in Belgium felt it was a courageous act of Freddy to make such a public testimony containing so many hard truths without allowing it to degenerate into an opportunity to swipe out at everyone around him.

The fact that there has never been any legal action brought against him by any of the characters featured in the book has only served to give more weight to the revelations. There have, of course, been denials from within the cycling fraternity since some would have preferred to see 'the lid stay on the pot,' but when writing the book, the co-authors consciously left any facts out of the book which could have been disproved.

Freddy Maertens continues to stand by everything he said in the book and has never wanted to or been made to withdraw a word of it. As far as he is concerned the book contains nothing but the truth.

Readers will have become only too aware of how pressing Maertens' financial worries became in the later years of his career and how he hoped that he would eventually turn the corner as he looked forward to a new start in retirement from professional cycling. It can be reported that Freddy is still working as a sales representative and exclusive distributor for the sports clothing company Assos, the job he had just taken up in 1988. His wife Carine works with him and trade is going very well for them both.

While this provides financial security for the Maertens family – Freddy, wife Carine and daughter Romy still live in their rented house in Rumbeke – the overall situation has not improved to any great degree.

Litigation concerning the winding-up of Flandria following the company's bankruptcy is still underway, although Freddy concedes that he is only one on a long list of creditors and will have to patiently wait and see if any of the monies owed to him will be paid. His other main financial concern, that of the tax office's claims on a great deal of outstanding money, may be resolved sooner, since the claim will shortly expire due to the time-lapse law involved. This, naturally, has given Maertens cause for optimism for the future.

He feels that there is less likelihood of riders facing the same sort of financial abuse that befell him during his career due to a larger degree of protection which professional riders can call on nowadays, and in his opinion it is just as well!

Although no longer actively involved in the sport, Maertens still follows the world of professional cycling closely; not surprisingly in view of the sporting associations of his job.

He feels that the style of racing has changed greatly since his days at the top, with a much narrower gap existing between the top men in a team and the domestiques. Now that the peloton is no longer controlled by one or two riders who stand out above the rest, the surprise wins occur more frequently and this, he feels, can bring a certain 'charm' to the sport. However, he is also concerned at the boring racing which tends to occur when a 'little fish' escapes on massive breakaways because the big men refuse to mount a chase after him. On the whole this has not been such a positive development according to Maertens.

Since his retirement there have been several changes within international professional cycling organisation on which he was asked to comment.

"Only time will tell if the ideas of Hein Verbruggen, chairman of the FICP, on modern racing are the right ones," is Maertens' view.

There is one tendency which has surfaced and which really annoys him. He feels each rider places too much emphasis on his own FICP points when, according to Freddy, cycling has always been a sport in which the sponsors' interests should be served by teams. For this reason he would like to see sponsors offer longer contracts to domestiques – 3 years for instance – and were this to happen, domestiques would be far more inclined to forego their own interests for those of their sponsor.

On being asked if he could foresee any potential world-beaters from his own country, as there were in his day, Freddy echoed the generally held view in Belgium at the moment that there is no-one among the current crop. He does, however, follow the performances of Johan Museeuw, since he rates him very highly for the way he is so frequently in the frame in the classics.

For the benefit of those of us who follow the sport in our own English-speaking countries we asked if he had any particular views on the development of cycling but he had to admit that it is difficult to follow results closely from Belgium, although he always looks for the outcome of stage races the world over through the media coverage available. He does, however, feel that cycling will continue to grow in popularity in the 'Anglo-Saxon' world.

Finally, when asked whether there were any plans to return to the sport in a more active way, we were greeted with an emphatic no! Freddy seems to be very content with his new career, particularly as it keeps him in contact with cycling news in general. He is clearly still very much in the public eye in his native country, thanks in part to the book, of course, and, as he says, he is always being asked for advice from young cyclists and is pleased to pass on his experience. Furthermore, he is in demand to act as guest of honour at races and sports meetings now and then, so the world of cycling is never far away from him. He has also met up again with Lomme Driessens, by chance, on a few occasions – even visiting his wife Maria when she was in hospital some time ago – and stresses that there is no ill-feeling at all between the two of them now.

While he and his family are well, we regrettably have to report that since the book was originally published his mother has passed away.

Cycling will always be in Freddy's blood, but now his own bike-riding is restricted to going out for a spin on a Sunday for relaxation. He is so busy with his work that anything more is out of the question!

Appendix: Freddy Maertens' 22 seasons as a cyclist

1966 (not affiliated): 1 victory.
During the Criterium of the Westhoek, in his home village of Lombardsijde, he won for the first time on 20th September.

1967 (not affiliated): 13 victories.
Thanks to his 12 stage victories, he was the overall winner of the Criterium of the Westhoek.

1968 (newcomer): 21 victories (and thus the WSC Torhout club champion) including the provincial championship at Helkijn.

1969 (junior): 22 victories.

1970 (junior): 43 victories (and once again WSC Torhout club champion) including the provincial championship at Ruddervoorde.

1971 (amateur): 21 victories including the national championship at Nandrin.
Top ten finishes
– 3rd in final classification in Tour of Algeria
– 2nd in world championship at Mendrisio

1972 (amateur and later professional): 30 victories as amateur and 1 as professional.
As an amateur, he won the provincial championship at Bavikhove. He made his debut as a professional with the Flandria-Beaulieu team on 1st October in Paris-Tours in which he finished 26th. On 5th October, he won his first race as a professional at Zwevezele.

1973 (Flandria-Carpenter-Shimano): 14 victories including:
– final victory in the Dunkirk Four Days (in which he won 1 stage)
– Scheldt Grand Prix (at Schoten)

Top ten finishes:
– 2nd in Tour of Flanders
– 5th in Ghent-Wevelgem
– 8th in Amstel Gold Race
– 5th in Paris-Roubaix
– 3rd in Rund um den Henninger Turm (at Frankfurt)
– 8th in national championship at Soumagne
– 2nd in world championship at Barcelona
Points classification:
– 1st in the Dunkirk Four Days

1974 (Flandria-Carpenter-Confortluxe): 33 victories including:
– overall victory in Tour of Andalusia (with 5 stage wins)
– overall victory in Tour of Belgium (with 4 stage wins although
the final stage victory and overall victory were later withdrawn)
– 1 stage win in the Dunkirk Four Days
– overall victory in Tour of Luxemburg (with 2 stage wins)
– provincial championships at Izegem
Top ten finishes:
– 8th in Het Volk
– 6th in Tirreno-Adriatico
– 9th in Milan-San Remo
– 7th in Paris-Roubaix
– 6th in Fleche Wallonne
– 4th in Amstel Gold Race
– 9th in Liège-Bastogne-Liège
– 4th in Rund um den Henninger Turm (at Frankfurt)
– 3rd in the Four Days at Dunkirk
– 5th in Midi-Libre
– 5th in Tours-Versailles
Points classification:
– 1st in Tour of Andalusia
– 1st in Tour of Belgium (later disqualified)
– 1st in the Dunkirk Four Days
– 1st in Tour of Luxemburg

1975 (Flandria-Carpenter-Confortluxe): 33 victories including:
– overall victory in the Tour of Andalusia (with 5 stage wins)
– 1 stage win in Paris-Nice
– overall victory in Tour of Belgium (with 1 stage win)

- Ghent-Wevelgem
- overall victory in the Dunkirk Four Days (with 1 stage win)
- 7 stage wins in Dauphiné Libéré
- Paris-Brussels
- Tours-Versailles

Top ten finishes:
- 9th in Milan-San Remo
- 2nd in Amstel Gold Race
- 8th in Tour of Flanders
- 6th in Paris-Roubaix
- 4th in Fleche Wallonne
- 4th in Rund um den Henninger Turm (at Frankfurt)
- 3rd in Scheldt Grand Prix (at Schoten)
- 5th in Tour of Lombardy
- 2nd in Baracchi Trophy

Points classification:
- 1st in Tour of Andalusia
- 1st in Tour of Belgium
- 1st in Dauphiné Libéré

1976 (Flandria-Velda-Westvlaams Vleesbedrijf): 54 victories including:
- 2 stage wins in Tour of Corsica
- 6 stage wins in Paris-Nice
- Amstel Gold Race
- Flèche Brabançonne
- 1 stage win in Tour of Belgium
- Ghent-Wevelgem
- Rund um den Henninger Turm (at Frankfurt)
- Championship of Zurich
- Dunkirk Four Days (with 1 stage win)
- 2 stage wins in Tour of Switzerland
- national championship at Dilsen
- 8 stage wins in Tour de France
- 2 stage wins in Tour of the Netherlands
- World Championship at Ostuni
- Grand Prix des Nations
- Barrachi Trophy
- Super Prestige winner

Top ten finishes:
– 4th in final classification in Paris-Nice 3rd in final classification in Tour of Belgium
– 5th in Tour of Flanders
– 3rd in Fleche Wallonne
– 2nd in Liège-Bastogne-Liège
– 7th in final classification in Tour of Switzerland
– 8th in final classification in Tour de France
– 8th in final classification in Tour of the Netherlands
– 4th in Paris-Brussels
Points classification:
– 1st in Tour de France
– 1st in Tour of the Netherlands

1977 (Flandria-Velda-Latina): 53 victories including:
– overall victory in Tour of Sardinia (with 1 stage win)
– Het Volk
– overall victory in Paris-Nice (with 5 stage wins)
– overall victory in Catalan Week (with 5 stage wins)
– Fleche Wallonne (later disqualified)
– 1 stage win in Tour of Belgium (later disqualified)
– overall victory in Tour of Spain (with 13 stage wins)
– 7 stage wins in Tour of Italy
– 1 stage win in Tour of Switzerland
– 1 stage win in Tour of the Netherlands
– overall victory in Tour of Catalonia (with 5 stage wins)
– Super Prestige winner
Top ten finishes:
– 5th in Milan-San Remo
– 2nd in Tour of Switzerland (later disqualified)
– 5th in Amstel Gold Race
– 9th in final classification in Tour of Belgium
– 3rd in Paris-Roubaix
– 5th in Liège-Bastogne-Liège
– 8th in Paris-Brussels
Points classification:
– 1st in Tour of Spain
– 1st in Tour of Catalonia

1978 (Flandria-Velda-Lano): 18 victories including:
– 1 stage win in Tour of Majorca
– Het Volk
– overall victory in the Dunkirk Four Days (with 2 stage wins)
– 1 stage win in Dauphiné Libéré
– 1 stage win in Tour of Switzerland
– 2 stage wins in Tour de France
Top ten finishes:
– 2nd in final classification in Tour of Majorca
– 4th in Amstel Gold Race
– 2nd in final classification in Tour of Belgium
– 8th in Tour of Flanders
– 9th in Ghent-Wevelgem
– 4th in Paris-Roubaix
– 9th in Liège-Bastogne-Liège
Points classification:
– 1st in Tour de France

1979 (Flandria-Ca va seul-Sunair): 2 victories.
Won two kermesse races in Belgium at Bredene and Wingene.

1980 (San Giacomo-Mobilli): 1 victory.
– The Chronostafetta at Montecatini Terme in Italy.

1981 (Boule D'Or Colnago): 11 victories including:
– 1 stage win in Ruta del Sol
– 5 stage wins in Tour de France
– World Championship in Prague
Top ten finishes:
– 7th in Milan-San Remo
Points classification:
– 1st in Tour de France

1982 (Boule D'Or- Colnago): no victories.
Top ten finishes:
– 9th in the De Panne Three Days

1983 (Masta-TeVeBlad-Concorde): 1 victory.
The kermesse at Hannut

1984 (AVP-Viditel; later Splendor): no victories.

1985 (Nikon-Elro: later Euro-Soap-Crack): 1 victory.
On 11th July he won for the last time in his career at Gistel.

1986 (Robland): no victories.

1987 (Robland): no victories.

Index

Riders

Rider continued

Jos Jacobs 67
Ward Janssens 112
Gerben Karstens 71
Sean Kelly 110, 137, 184
Martin Kemps 176
Gerrie Knetemann 47, 110, 141
Krzeszowiec 24
Hennie Kuiper 32, 54, 65
Eric Leman 28, 39, 48
Norbert Lesage 11
Roland Liboton 30
Eric Loder 73
Marc (Maertens) 5, 6, 7, 16, 79,
  151, 152, 161, 168, 169, 170
René Maertens 6, 10
Bernard Maertens 6
Geert Malfait 131
Lieven Malfait 110
René Martens 112
Giuseppe Martinelli 120
Palmiro Masciarelli 145
Eddy Merckx 9, 16, 24, 27, 28,
  37, 38, 39, 40, 41, 42, 43, 44,
  47, 50, 51, 52, 54, 62, 66, 67,
  78, 79, 80, 81, 82, 83, 86, 87,
  91, 92, 98, 106, 112, 123, 147,
  164, 170, 186
Jean-Pierre Monseré 18, 19,
  20, 23, 24, 26, 54, 76, 134
Francesco Moser 62, 65, 79,
  80, 82, 83, 87, 93, 95, 98, 103,
  104, 110, 122, 145, 170
Wim Myngheer 110
Ludo Noels 26
Luis Ocana 40, 41, 71
Marcel Omloop 34
Regis Ovion 27
Luc Pels 14
Frits Pirard 131

Eddy Planckaert 138, 152, 158
Walter Planckaert 36, 62, 79,
  107, 138, 158
Michel Pollentier 1, 3, 11, 13,
  15, 34, 36, 37, 38, 46, 47, 48,
  54, 55, 58, 60, 67, 68, 69, 70,
  72, 74, 79, 80, 82, 93, 94, 95,
  96, 97, 99, 103, 104, 105, 106,
  107, 108, 109, 110, 118, 122,
  123, 124, 129, 130, 150, 152,
  157, 162, 163, 168
Raymond Poulidor 39
Cees Priem 32
Jan Raas 47, 104, 107, 122
Stephen Roche 184
Rudy Rogiers 144
Giussepe Saronni 145, 146, 164
Roy Schuiten 51, 82
Karel Sels 18
Patrick Sercu 84
Marc Sergeant 150, 152
Johny Soenens 14
Roger Swerts 48
Ryszard Szurkowski 24, 27
William Tackaert 163, 164
Willy Teirlinck 88
Bernard Thevenet 51
Didi Thurau 98, 141
Marcel Tinazzi 141
Staf Van Cauter 25, 27
Peter Van De Knoop 176
Jean-Luc Vandenbroucke 67
Antoon van den Bunder 11
Eric Vanderaerden 133, 152
Ludo van der Linden 14, 25, 27,
  31, 145
Marcel Vanderslagmolen 161
Ludo Vandromme 13

Places in Belgium

Overseas places

Races/Tours

Acht van Brasschaat 43, 81, 91
Acht van Chaam 79
Tour of Algeria 23, 24, 29
Amstel Gold Race 39, 62, 103,
175
Tour of Andalusia (see also
Ruta del Sol) 46, 52, 74
Annual Fair Grand Prix 19
Antwerp Six Days 84, 154
Tour de l'Aude 134, 160
Baracchi Trophy 3, 53, 74, 82
Belgian Championship 13, 14,
18, 23, 39, 88, 106, 134
For the following venues see
under Belgian places.
– 1969 Nandrin
– 1970 Meulebeke
– 1971 Nandrin
– 1973 Soumagne
– 1976 Dilsen
– 1977 Yvoir
– 1978 Vielsalm
– 1981 Putte
– 1982 Tertre
Belgian Track Championships
84
Tour of Belgium 48, 52, 88, 171
Tour of Campania 122
Catalan Week 85, 113
Tour of Catalonia 56, 98
Châteaulin 81
Chronostafetta 121
Circuit of the Flemish
Ardennes 113, 131, 184
Coastal Arrow Race 133
Cordenone 82
Criterium of the Westhoek 7,
10, 11, 12, 13, 34, 151
Dauphiné Libéré 52, 60

De Panne Three Days 127,
158, 183
Dunkirk Four Days 39, 66,
106, 132
E3 Race (Harelbeke) 103, 104
La Fausto Coppi 184
Championship of Flanders 36
Tour of Flanders 39, 52, 60, 62,
63, 65, 78, 85, 86, 87, 98, 104,
113, 122, 130, 131, 132, 158
Flèche Brabançonne 62
Flèche Wallonne 47, 48, 65, 87,
98, 113, 131
Tour de France 38, 40, 49, 50,
53, 57, 61, 64, 67, 69, 71, 75,
78, 84, 85, 94, 101, 102, 103,
106, 107, 108, 109, 134, 135,
136, 139, 140, 141, 148, 157,
158, 160, 161, 162, 183
Ganshoren-Meulebeke Race
105
Tour of Germany 141
Ghent Six Days 118
Ghent-Wevelgem 39, 48, 52,
64, 104, 113, 130, 132, 168,
169, 182
Gippingen (Switz.) 44
Giro (see Tour of Italy)
Grand-Prix Eddy Merckx 148
Grand-Prix Karel van
Wijnendaele 30
Grand-Prix of Camaiore 123
Grand-Prix of Laigueglia 84,
121
Grand-Prix of Malaga 170
Grand-Prix des Nations
(Angers) 55, 68, 71, 82, 83,
98, 71, 101, 102
Grape Race (Overijse) 141, 142

Races continued

Grenoble Six Days 34
Henninger Turm (Rund um dem) 39, 47, 66, 72, 132, 153, 160
Het Volk (Ghent-Ghent) 30, 62, 103, 121, 131, 158
Tour of Italy (Giro) 67, 84, 85, 88, 93, 94, 95, 99, 106, 113, 122, 141
Kellogg's races 184
Liège-Bastogne-Liège 48, 65, 88, 104, 159
Tour of Lombardy 61, 98, 118
Longchamps 99
Maffle-Mouscron-Maffle 142
Majorca Two Days 103
Midi Libre 53, 134, 137, 160
Tour of the Midi Pyrenées 159
Milan-San Remo 48, 62, 113, 121, 131, 158, 174, 175, 176, 177
Milan Six Days 60, 84, 121, 154
Montjuich Hill-Climb 106, 153 (see also World Championship, Barcelona 1973)
Tour of Morocco 29
Tour of the Netherlands 79, 80
Tour de l'Oise 132
Olympic Games 1972 – 28, 30, 31, 33
– Munich 28, 29, 30, 31, 32, 33
Paris-Brussels 35, 48, 54, 98, 106, 149, 184
Paris-Nice 62, 69, 70, 85, 90, 121, 131
Paris-Roubaix 15, 37, 39, 48, 52, 65, 88, 104, 106, 113, 132, 160
Paris-Tours 12, 34

Rotterdam Six Days 154
Ruta del Sol (see also Tour of Andalusia) 131, 152, 155, 156, 170
Tour of Sardinia 121
Scheldt Grand-Prix 117
Seillans-Draguignan 103
Sombreffe-Charleroi 114
Tour of Switzerland 67, 85, 96, 106
Tirreno-Adriatico 156, 158
Tours-Versailles 48, 54
Trophée Gan 119
Trophée Pantalica 122
Villafranca 82
Voghern 82
Vuelta (Tour of Spain) 67, 84, 85, 94, 99, 157
West Flemish Championship 13, 30
William Tell Tour 31
World Championships 41, 164, 186
1970 – Mallory Park 18
1971 – Mendrisio 25, 26, 27, 28, 31
1973 – Barcelona 39, 40, 41, 43, 44, 50, 72, 91
Montjuich 39, 41, 91
1974 – Montreal 50, 51
1975 – Yvoir – see Belgium
1976 – Ostuni 79, 81, 82, 98, 145, 147, 148, 153, 154
1977 – San Cristobal 56, 68, 97, 98
1978 – Nürburgring 110
1979 – Valkenburg 117

Races continued

Locations during stage races

Tour de France

Ruta del Sol

Giro

Vuelta

Others

Miscellaneous